#SmartCustody

Use of Advanced Cryptographic Tools to Improve the Care, Maintenance, Control, and Protection of Digital Assets

v1.01 - 2019-06-19

Christopher Allen and Shannon Appelcline

ISBN 978-1-7340637-0-7

Contents

Disclaimer

The information below is intended to inform a set of best practices. It may not address risks specific to your situation, and if it does not, you should modify appropriately. While this information may inform best practices, there is no guarantee that following this advice will sufficiently ensure the security of your digital assets. In addition, this information is only a window on best practices at a specific moment in time. Be aware that the Bitcoin & blockchain ecosystems may have evolved and the risk assessments of specific products may have changed since the publication of this draft. In other words: be cautious, be careful, and be aware of the current Bitcoin & blockchain landscape before you use this information.

Credits

Lead Authors: Christopher Allen @ChristopherA[1], Shannon Appelcline @Appelcline[2]

Additional Contributors: Bryan Bishop @kanzure[3] (Adversaries, Risk Modeling), Greg Maxwell (Adversaries)

Reviewers: Ferdinando Maria Ametrano, Nicolas Bacca @LedgerHQ[4], Bryan Bishop @kanzure[5], Miron C., Angus Champion de Crespigny @anguschampion[6], Tuur Deemester @TuurDemeester[7], Ryan Grant, Greg Maxwell, Pamela Morgan @pamelawjd[8], Karim Nassar @karimofthecrop[9], Adam Shostack @adamshostack[10], Peter Todd @peterktodd[11], Henk van Cann, Jonathan Wilkins, Glenn Willen @gwillen[12]

Also, thanks to 3Blue1Brown who has created an excellent YouTube video[13] on how to think about large numbers. We borrowed his process, but adapted it in our own way. Any understanding comes from his approach, while any mistakes in calculation are ours.

---

[1] https://twitter.com/ChristopherA
[2] https://twitter.com/Appelcline
[3] https://twitter.com/kanzure
[4] https://twitter.com/LedgerHQ
[5] https://twitter.com/kanzure
[6] https://twitter.com/AngusChampion
[7] https://twitter.com/TuurDemeester
[8] https://twitter.com/pamelawjd
[9] https://twitter.com/karimofthecrop
[10] https://twitter.com/adamshostack
[11] https://twitter.com/peterktodd
[12] https://twitter.com/gwillen
[13] https://www.youtube.com/watch?v=S9JGmA5_unY

The #SmartCustody Team

#SmartCustody[14] is a project of Blockchain Commons[15], which supports blockchain infrastructure, internet security, and cryptographic research.

The leads for these #SmartCustody efforts are Christopher Allen (@ChristopherA[16]) and Shannon Appelcline (@Appelcline[17]). For more information see Author Bios at end of this book.

The procedures and contents of this white paper have been comprehensively peer-reviewed by a number of experts in the digital-asset ecosystem, including contributors to open-source project like Bitcoin Core and The Glacier Project[18], employees of blockchain technology companies like Blockstream, Ledger, and Tokensoft, and attorneys from a variety of disciplines. We expect to iterate these procedures and update this document regularly as new digital asset technologies and best practices become mature.

Copyright & Contributing

Unless otherwise noted, the contents of this book are Copyright 2017-2019 by Blockchain Commons and are licensed CC-BY-SA[19]

Please give attribution by linking to the https://www.SmartCustody.com[20] website.

Any questions or issues concerning this white paper or contributions of updates via pull requests can be made via our Github repository at https://github.com/BlockchainCommons/SmartCustodyBook[21].

---

[14]https://www.SmartCustody.com
[15]https://www.BlockchainCommons.com
[16]https://twitter.com/ChristopherA
[17]https://twitter.com/Appelcline
[18]https://glacierprotocol.org/
[19]https://creativecommons.org/licenses/by-sa/4.0/
[20]https://www.SmartCustody.com
[21]https://github.com/BlockchainCommons/SmartCustodyBook

Sponsors

The mission of the Blockchain Commons is to support blockchain infrastructure and the broader security industry through cryptographic research, cryptographic & privacy protocol implementations, architecture & code reviews, industry standards, and supportive documentation. We are a "not-for-profit" benefit corporation, with a strong commitment to open source and a defensive patent strategy.

Our mission is funded by people like you: your personal or corporate patronage can help the Commons to accomplish its goals. Together, we can expand and improve the blockchain infrastructure that's used by our entire industry, and with your gift, we can remain independent while doing so.

The following parties have contributed to this project in order to make it freely available to the public and to support continued updates as technology changes. If you're interested in sponsoring this or other Blockchain Commons projects, contact ChristopherA[22]. You can also make a one-time contribution via our Support #SmartCustody Book Crowdfunding[23] page.

Sustaining Patrons

Sustaining patrons have made an ongoing commitment of funds for the support of Blockchain Commons and/or its #SmartCustody work.

Digital Contract Design[24] creates contracts with trust minimization. They engage in Contract Design to show how contracts could be made more reliable; they offer Threat Analysis to demonstrate how well contract design holds up in an adversarial setting; and they work with the W3C Credentials Community Group and Rebooting Web-of-Trust community to provide a Self-Sovereign Identity Wallet.

HTC Exodus[25] is the product of HTC, who brings brilliance to life through leading innovation in smart mobile device and experience design. Beginning with a vision to put a personal computer in the palm of our customers' hands, they have led the way in the evolution from palm PC to smartphone. Their goal for the Exodus blockchain phone is to rebuild trust, one phone at a time.

---

[22]mailto:ChristopherA@blockchaincommons.com
[23]https://btcpay.blockchaincommons.com/apps/r6JPAMd5pUed6x4iQChstkkUx3q/crowdfund
[24]https://contract.design
[25]https://www.htcexodus.com/eu/

Project Sponsors

Project sponsors have donated funds specifically for the creation of this #SmartCustody book.

Adamant Capital[26] believes that Bitcoin is retooling the financial industry. They run Adamant Fund I, a Bitcoin Alpha fund. Their mission is to responsibly outperform Bitcoin in a tax-efficient manner. Their vision is to build on Bitcoin as a collateral asset, as a basis for lending, as a financial benchmark, and as a developing technology.

Beam Privacy[27] is a scalable confidential cryptocurrency: a Mimblewimble implementation. It completely conceals the values and metadata of transactions, in a prunable way which also reduces bloating on the blockchain. In addition to enhanced privacy and fungibility, this allows for much greater scalability. Beam's emphasis is on privacy, scalability, and usability. Download their wallet[28] to try it out.

Blockchainbird[29] is a free and open source software toolset with a manual to build an extra guarantee layer on existing database systems. It is free to use and adapt to your own needs.

Smartphones and smart custody arranged? Then Bird gives wings to projects that are labeled as blockchain, but can in fact be implemented with databases.

Catallaxy[30] develops products and services in the domain of finance and accounting. The group of technology experts in cryptography, blockchain, data science and artificial intelligence develops solutions that can help build trust in the digital economy. Based in Montréal, Catallaxy is a subsidiary of Raymond Chabot Grant Thornton[31], a professional services firm, also a member firm of Grant Thornton International Ltd[32].

---

[26] https://www.adamantcapitalfund.com/
[27] https://beam.mw
[28] https://beam.mw/downloads
[29] https://github.com/blockchainbird/bird
[30] https://catallaxy.rcgt.com/en/
[31] https://www.rcgt.com/en/
[32] https://www.grantthornton.global/en/

Hardcore Fund[33] is a nonprofit organization backed by hardcore bitcoiners. We donate to those who contribute to the Bitcoin ecosystem independently as an individual, a team or a nonprofit project. Our mission is to diversify the current bitcoin developement funding landscape and cover neutral developers from all over the world. The fund is currently run and managed by Kevin Pan and Dovey Wan

Ledger[34] develops security and infrastructure solutions for cryptocurrencies, as well as blockchain applications for individuals and companies, by leveraging a distinctive, proprietary technology. Their Ledger Nano S and the touchscreen Ledger Blue can both directly support 23 cryptocurrencies – and dozens more via third party applications.

Unchained Capital[35] is a new kind of financial services company. They are the first collaborative asset management firm that offers loans and vaults for your Bitcoin. It was founded by people who believe that cryptocurrencies have the potential to change the world but only if they're useful. They set out to build financial products for long-term crypto-investors to get more value from their assets today and in the future.

Winstead[36] is a law firm whose Fintech, Cryptocurrencies & Emerging Technologies team counsels clients on structuring digital asset transactions – from trading cryptocurrencies directly; participating in token launches; secondary trading of tokens; acquiring digital asset exposure through equity vehicles and derivatives; or making more traditional venture capital or other investments in companies building protocols, trading platforms other infrastructure.

---

[33]https://hardcore.fund/
[34]https://www.ledger.com/
[35]https://www.unchained-capital.com/
[36]https://www.winstead.com/Practices/Corporate-SecuritiesMA/Fintech-Cryptocurrencies-Emerging-Technologies

In-Kind Sponsors

In-kind sponsors have provided material such as books or hardware devices that were distributed at a #SmartCustody event or have provided space for an event.

Blockstream[37] has a mission to create the financial infrastructure of the future. They build crypto-financial infrastructure based on Bitcoin, the most robust and secure blockchain. Applying cutting-edge cryptography and security engineering, they are building the products and networks that make financial markets more efficient by reducing reliance on trust.

Cryptoasset Inheritance Planning[38] **by Pamela Morgan** is a clear blueprint to inheritance planning for those holding cryptocurrency, tokens, crypto-collectibles, and other cryptoassets. Since 2015, Pamela has educated thousands of cryptocurrency owners around the world about why inheritance planning for cryptoassets matters and how to do it in a secure, usable, resilient, and efficient manner.

CryptoTag[39] is a crypto security company from Amsterdam. They believe cryptocurrencies and blockchain will make our society a better place. They are a security company whose customers count on them to be there when all the other layers of security, like hardware and software layers, fail.

---

[37]https://blockstream.com/
[38]https://t.co/hsLxiZdQya
[39]https://cryptotag.io/

Other Financial Contributors

Thanks to the following who have offered financial contributions to the #SmartCustody project in order to make it freely available to the public and to support continued updates as the technology changes.

- **Andreas M. Antonopoulos**
- **Anonymous (x3)**
- **Gabriele Domenichini**
- **Frederic Meyer**
- **David Strayhorn**

If you would like to support this project and be added to this list of financial contributors, you can do so via the #SmartCustody Book Crowdfunding[40] page on our BTCPay[41] server (also available via the QR code below). You can also contact ChristopherA[42] directly, particularly if you're interested in making a larger or continuing contribution.

---

[40]https://btcpay.blockchaincommons.com/apps/r6JPAMd5pUed6x4iQChstkkUx3q/crowdfund
[41]https://btcpay.blockchaincommons.com/
[42]mailto:ChristopherA@blockchaincommons.com

Foreword

The Key Management of Digital Assets

by Christopher Allen

I first became fascinated by the possibilities offered by public key cryptography when reading about the RSA algorithm in the early '90s. However, I didn't really start to deal with the problems of key management of my own large large cryptographic keys until the launch of PGP in 1992.

Over those early years I've lost quite a few of my keys, mostly due to overly complex passwords that I thought I could remember. As I got better at that, I lost still more due to accidently erased folders or hard drives and a few others due to bitrot. I also got very early digital currency when I did some consulting with Digicash, but not only did I never cash it out, I can't run the software anymore, as the servers it required have been gone for over a decade.

The oldest keypair that I still have the private key for is now over 20 years old (ChristopherA@consensus.com ABB2B7CEE0983CD798D4266CCA7CBC1873262B3A DSA-1024 created 1998-12-09). I kept it for a long time due to the old, sentimental web-of-trust attestations associated with it, such as those from the founders of PGP and many early members of the SSL/TLS community, but I revoked it in 2015 as it was getting out-of-date with current security standards.

This history gives me some perspective when it comes to the protection and management of keys for digital assets. Bitcoin in particular made some some massive improvements to the ability to manage lots of keys. However, problems with managing digital assets still exist: despite these improvements, I have seen my own colleagues lose millions of dollars in early bitcoin.

Last year I surveyed a number of my professional colleagues in both the Bitcoin and Ethereum communities about their personal digital key management and custody practices. Despite the publication of very strong advice with projects like The Glacier Project, many of them had not

actually implemented anything close to that level of sophistication. In most cases it was "Perfection is the Enemy of the Good" keeping them from doing what they know are better practices. Some even admitted that they were still using an old paper wallet or had a laptop locked up in their attic. Given the large destructive fires in California over the last several years, this worried me.

When talking my colleagues I also learned that many didn't want to share their best practices publically for operational security (op-sec) reasons, believing that it might put them at risk for attack or even physical coercion. Some of this is legitimate concern, especially for those living outside of the US, but to a certain extent I find in my work that "security by obscurity" is often a bad practice. Thus, the first version of the smart-custody scenarios included in this book are based on my own approach and methods, which I then shared with my professional colleagues for improvements.

Christopher Allen
@ChristopherA

Do you store your digital asset keys encrypted or plaintext?

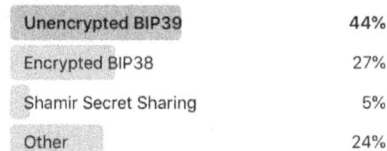

Unencrypted BIP39	44%
Encrypted BIP38	27%
Shamir Secret Sharing	5%
Other	24%

41 votes · Final results

When I started to share these scenarios outside the professional community, I discovered that there were some very different ways of thinking about digital asset risk that kept people from adapting them for their own needs. So I've also explained my own approach here, to encourage adoption. It's an approach to risk modeling that is meant to balance the "perfection" problem and to engender a general cryptographer-oriented way of thinking from an "adversarial" perspective.

This topic is evolving rapidly, and many things will likely change over time, but I hope that this book will help you to think differently about your digital assets and to know a bit more about how to get started, how to ask smart questions, and how to evolve your own procedures over time.

We are very open to your feedback and look forward to learning from you what we missed.

–Christopher Allen

Preface to the Book

This is a book about #SmartCustody[43], which we define as:

> *"The use of advanced cryptographic tools to improve the care, maintenance, control, and protection of digital assets."*

There are many ways to address #SmartCustody. This book offers procedural solutions: it teaches you to model the risks to your digital assets using a methodology where you assess vulnerabilities in a systematic way, then address them. Two major building blocks will help you in doing so: a cold-storage scenario for protecting your less-used digital assets; and a set of adversaries, which are personifications of the risks you may face.

This book initially focuses on the simplest #SmartCustody scenarios, concentrating on self-custody, where someone is holding their own digital assets. But many cryptocurrency afficiandos will be more interested in scenarios where they are holding assets for clients. This same risk modeling methodology may be applied to these more complex scenarios, as is detailed in the latter part of this book.

Why Cold Storage?

Cold storage is primarily intended for digital-asset custodians who do not actively trade their digital assets. It offers a high level of protection for digital assets, because keys are secured offline or in hardware and *should never be on networked computers.*

However, cold storage should be considered as an option for *everyone* who is managing digital assets. It can be the secure foundation for a more complex scenario that also involves hot wallets, offering the maximum security for whatever percentage of funds don't need to be actively available at all times.

A few questions can help you determine if you can move some of your funds from hot wallets to cold storage:

1. How much readily available liquidity do you need?
2. How often are you moving your digital assets?
3. How often are you exchanging your digital assets?

---

[43]https://www.SmartCustody.com

After you answer these questions, you may discover that you don't actually need all of your funds to be always available. The remainder should then be moved off of exchanges into a cold-storage scenario, and the following can provide a model for that.

Even if you determine that all of your funds must remain hot, our cold-storage scenario still suggests a variety of best practices for managing digital-asset keys, and does so in the context of risks and adversaries that can be used to model other scenarios.

About the #SmartCustody Project

#SmartCustody is a Blockchain Commons project with two goals:

- To raise the bar on best practices for digital-asset custodianship by building a greater understanding of different custody use cases, risk models, and adversary threats; and
- To prepare for new custody technologies that break old models for custodianship.

To accomplish these goals, we are creating a series of best-practices documents, offering a series of different workshops on these topics, and collaborating with cryptographic industry and regulatory stakeholders to establish standards, improve best practices, and create new cryptographic key-management and custody technologies.

This book is our first best-practices document.

To be informed of the release of future best-practices and other educational documents and to learn about future workshops, subscribe to our email newsletter at https://tinyletter.com/SmartCustody[44].

---

[44]https://tinyletter.com/SmartCustody

Introduction: The Power of Randomness

Why we do what we do

Version: 2019-06-27 Release 1.0.0

Introduction to Randomness

Cryptographers love randomness.

They love numbers that are entirely unpredictable, where there's an equal probability that any number will be selected, and where that selection occurs independently of anything else. It creates a *secret*, which is the heart of cryptography.

Here's why you should love those random numbers too.

The Power of Large Numbers

Imagine your Bitcoin (or other digital assets) as being held in a near-infinite set of lockers. Anyone can see what's in a locker, and anyone can put money in a locker, but each locker is secured with a (secret) combination, and only the person with the combination can retrieve the money.

One standard type of combination lock has four digits that each run from 0 to 9. That creates 10^4 combinations or 10,000 possible secrets. Here's where the randomness comes in: if the combination is actually unpredictable, then it can only be broken by someone running through all the possible combinations: 0000, 0001, 0002, etc. If they could test a number a second, they'd break the combination in at most three hours (and on average, in an hour and a half).

Clearly, that's not a sufficient secret to protect actual money (like cryptocurrencies), especially when attackers can test numbers covertly (over the internet). For that, you need a much larger secret number.

The Weakness of Passwords

"So," you might say. "Does that mean that I can use a password as a secret for protecting my digital assets? Then I can keep it in my head." Unfortunately, there are multiple problems with this methodology. First, a "brain wallet" is innately prone to failure; worse, there won't be any way for your heirs or descendants to reclaim your digital assets. However, one more sobering fact makes this methodology even more problematic: traditional passwords are no longer secure.

Theoretically an eight-character password contains 64 bits of randomness[45], but that turns out not to be the case in reality. That's because any character in a password is likely to be drawn from the 100 or so characters available on a standard keyboard: that immediately drops the 8 bits of randomness for each character down to 6 or 7, which would be 48 to 56 bits total for an eight-character password. But, passwords are worse than that. They tend to be arranged into words, and they tend to use standard substitutions, which makes them even less secure; like that four-digit locker combination, any short-to-medium-length password can be broken today in a fairly short amount of time!

The *zxcvbn*[46] *interactive password demo*[47] support the testing of passwords, with results shown for computers of various powers. Obviously *real* passwords should not be tested on any internet service, but the following benchmarks for entirely random passwords of different lengths are instructive. Each entry shows how long the password would take to crack given a machine that could make 10B (billion) guesses a second, which turns out to be a *realistic goal*[48]:

- 5 characters (58T%n): less than a second
- 8 characters (lVA#6jx6): less than a second
- 12 characters (G%6L3Y!5cvjC): 2 minutes
- 16 characters (g0oY!yXZg2Emn#3z): 12 days
- 18 characters (K1cAhiQ00I@Ol!vvvK): 1 year
- 20 characters (EoQ7^#y1xR^WeQeqdst$): centuries

And that's why you're not going to be brain-walleting a password for your digital assets: there's not enough randomness in a password for it to be an unguessable secret unless it's very long and fundamentally impossible to memorize. Oh, you could use an alternative like the *EFF's randomphrase list*[49], which allows you to get the equivalent of 77 bits of protection with six seven-character words. But even in these situations, you're unlikely to manage more than 80 bits of entropy, which is the absolute minimum you'd want in the current day and age.

At the moment, 80 bits of protection (the equivalent of that EFF randomphrase or another long password) are theoretically safe under any likely cracking scenario ... but the Bitcoin mining network

---

[45]A "bit of randomness" is the standard way to measure the strength of a random number. It's a single digit that can be set to either a "1" or a "0". 64 bits of randomness is therefore 64 digits that can each be set to either a "1" or a "0". That may not sound like a lot, but every bit you add doubles the possibilities: there are thus two options for a one-bit number ("0", "1"), four for a two-bit number ("00", "01", "10", "11"), eight for a three-bit number, etc. It quickly adds up.

[46]https://github.com/dropbox/zxcvbn/blob/master/README.md

[47]https://lowe.github.io/tryzxcvbn/

[48]https://arstechnica.com/information-technology/2012/12/25-gpu-cluster-cracks-every-standard-windows-password-in-6-hours/

[49]https://www.eff.org/deeplinks/2016/07/new-wordlists-random-passphrases

as a group actually passed the ability to make 2^80 guesses in a year at the end of 2013 and has *peaked at closer to 2^92*[50]. Though it's unlikely that someone could put together that much computing power to break a single key, that amount of computer power does already exist on Earth, and we wouldn't want our assets' safety lying so near the ever-advancing line of what can be broken.

Which is why it's fortunate that Bitcoin's virtual combination lock isn't 80 bits long, but rather 256.

The Power of 2^256

A 256-bit private key is a string of 256 ones or zeros, which, requiring 2^256 guesses to step through all of the possibilities, but that doesn't illustrate the whole scope of the number. We can bring it down to Earth by breaking it down as:

2^32 * 2^32 * 2^32 * 2^32 * 2^32 * 2^32 * 2^32 * 2^32

And since 2^32 is a bit more than four billion, this is about the same as:

4B * 4B * 4B * 4B * 4B * 4B * 4B * 4B

So, how hard is that to crack?

The Amazon Example

Amazon's exciting new 3.16xlarge cloud computer, which costs $25/hour to operate, can compute about 6 billion hashes a second. That only resolves one of those 2^32 multipliers, leaving seven to deal with:

(4B * 1.5 = 3.16xlarge computing power) *
⅔ * 4B * 4B * 4B * 4B * 4B * 4B * 4B

Perhaps we can do better by spending more money: with 21 trillion hashes in an hour costing $25, the overall cost of using the 3.16xlarge is about $1 for each thousand billion hashes. Multiply that by the eighty thousand billion dollars circulating in fiat currency, and you can run eighty million billion billion hashes before you bankrupt the whole world.

At this point, you've come up with a way to crack an 80-bit secret without using the entire Bitcoin mining network for a year. But, it's still nowhere near what you need to figure out that 256-bit Bitcoin secret, where you're still working on that third 2^32 multiplier, with five more to go!

Clearly we have to look beyond the global money supply out into the whole universe to do better.

---

[50]https://crypto.stackexchange.com/questions/13299/is-80-bits-of-key-size-considered-safe-against-brute-force-attacks/13305#13305

The Universal Example

Let's take an alternate route and instead consider the entire mining power of the Bitcoin network. That's been running about 40E in 2019, which is 40 billion billion hashes per second, or 6 billion times as much power as that single 3.16xlarge computer. This deals with two of the 2^32s required to crack a Bitcoin private key, but only by using up what may be the most powerful computer network on modern-day Earth.

(4B * 4B * 3 = Bitcoin mining power) *
⅓ * 4B * 4B * 4B * 4B * 4B * 4B

There are 7.7 billion people on Earth, so let's give every one of them a magic computer that has the entire power of the current Bitcoin mining network:

(4B * 4B * 3 = Bitcoin mining power) *
(4B * 2 = population of Earth) *
⅓ * ½ * 4B * 4B * 4B * 4B * 4B

There are 250 billion stars in the Milky Way (plus or minus 150 billion), so let's give every star an Earth-like planet where everyone is running magic computers:

(4B * 4B * 3 = Bitcoin mining power) *
(4B * 2 = population of Earth) *
(4B * 62 = stars in the Milky Way) *
1/3 * 1/2 * 1/62 * 4B * 4B * 4B * 4B

There are at least 200 billion galaxies in the universe:

(4B * 4B * 3 = Bitcoin mining power) *
(4B * 2 = population of Earth) *
(4B * 62 = stars in the Milky Way) *
(4B * 50 = galaxies in the universe) *
1/3 * 1/2 * 1/62 * 1/50 * 4B * 4B * 4B

And finally, it's been 13.7 billion years since the Big Bang, which is 432 million billion seconds.

(4B * 4B * 3 = Bitcoin mining power) *
(4B * 2 = population of Earth) *
(4B * 62 = stars in the Milky Way) *

(4B * 50 = galaxies in the universe) *

(4B * 108M = lifetime of the universe) *

1/3 * 1/2 * 1/62 * 1/50 * 1/108M * 4B * 4B

If you rearrange the fractions, what's left is:

1/500 * 1/4B * 4B * 4B

Or:

1/500 * 4B

Or:

8M

In other words, in order to crack a 256-bit secret by guessing all of the possible combinations in a Bitcoin private key, you'd have to have every star in the whole universe have an Earth-like planet where every person had their own complete Bitcoin mining network, and they'd all have to calculate for the entire lifetime of the universe, and then they'd have to do that 8 million more times!

Lucky you, on average you'll find the key in half of that, or 4 million times!

Bruce Schneier takes another approach in his *Applied Cryptography* (pages 157-158), describing how it would take channeling the entire power of a supernova just to cycle a single 219-bit counter through all of its permutations, making an attack on a 256-bit key not just chronologically infeasible, but energetically infeasible too.

Which is why cryptographers like randomness for protecting their secrets.

(And why the 256-bit private key is a lot better than your 12- or 16-character password.)

The Power of 2^160

Actually, the power of that 256-bit private key is so huge that Bitcoin itself doesn't use all of it. It instead hashes the public key of its keypair down to a 160-bit Bitcoin address. This *does* decrease the security, because now there are many collisions when converting from that 256-bit keyspace to this smaller 160-bit hashspace. But the number is still so hugely large that it doesn't matter.

2^{160} is only:

2^32 * 2^32 * 2^32 * 2^32 * 2^32

But that still means:

(4B * 4B * 3 = Bitcoin mining power) *

(4B * 2 = population of Earth) *

(4B * 108M = lifetime of the universe) *

1/3 * 1/2 * 1/108M * 4B

Or:

(4B * 4B * 3 = Bitcoin mining power) *

(4B * 2 = population of Earth) *

(4B * 108M = lifetime of the universe) *

6172

To break a 160-bit hash would require everyone on the Earth to have a computer with the power of the Bitcoin mining network and to run for six thousand times the lifetime of the universe.

Note that the reduction from the 256-bit private key to the 160-bit hash is not a requirement of Bitcoin (or any similar digital-asset system). It's simply how Bitcoin does things right now, as part of a balance between minimizing storage space while maintaining security that's at the moment well, well past borderline or reasonable protection

The Danger of Randomness

However, randomness isn't easy.

Humans are very bad at picking random numbers. Multiple studies have shown that *playing rock-scissors-paper is somewhat predictable*[51], and that's just humans picking among three numbers. Picking larger random number isn't any easier (quite the contrary).

And computers aren't much better at picking random numbers. In fact, they literally can't. To generate a pseudo-random number, a computer needs to start off with a random number as a seed, which creates a chicken and egg problem. There are certainly ways to resolve this, from the simple idea of seeding a pseudo-random number generator off of the current time to creating true randomness using stochastic natural processes such as thermal noise.

But, it's tough. And it's easy to mess up.

Here's another sobering reality: if a computer process messes up a single bit, then the number of possible guesses is reduced by half. And it doesn't tend to be just a single bit that's messed up! When we were doing security reviews of SSL products in the '90s, we found that about half the products failed the review due to a failure of randomness! Sometimes it's due to programming errors that entirely eliminate randomness, sometimes it's due to reuse of randomness (which of course isn't

[51]https://www.psychologytoday.com/us/blog/the-blame-game/201504/the-surprising-psychology-rock-paper-scissors

random), and sometimes it's due to leaked bits that someone else might know. Every one of these errors *substantially* reduces the randomness: the number of guesses might be reduced by 10x or 100x *or 10 billion times* or zeroed out all together!

So, cryptographers love randomness. But, randomness is hard and needs to be generated carefully.

The Core of Custody

This #SmartCustody book don't actually talk about *directly* protecting your cryptocurrency: your private key does that all on its own. In fact, everything that you do with cryptography, from protecting digital assets to signing digital documents, ultimately goes back to that secret. It doesn't matter if that number is part of public-key cryptography or a classic symmetric key cryptography system; in either case, the number protects your assets.

What this book instead teaches is how to protect that number, both by keeping it safe and only entrusting it to safe devices: so that you don't lose your secret, misuse it, or have it stolen.

That's all that smart custody is.

Part One: Risk Modeling

After that introduction, welcome to the core of #SmartCustody, where we talk about how to secure digital assets.

The heart of this #SmartCustody course is a system of **Risk Modeling**, which allows you to assess the vulnerabilities of your own digital assets, then resolve those vulnerabilities using a system of building blocks that we provide. This first Part explains how the the risk modeling works. The building blocks that are used by this risk modeling system, a cold storage self-custody system and a long detailing of adversaries, then appear in **Part Two** of this book.

Chapter One: Risk Modeling

Managing storage & transaction vulnerabilities

Version: 2019-07-05 1.0.0

Introduction to Risk Modeling

There are many risks in the world of digital assets. If you store your private keys insecurely, you could be burgled or hacked. If criminals know that you hold cryptocurrency funds, you could be kidnapped or threatened. If you are careless or unlucky, you could lose your private keys to misadventure, disaster, or even just the miscopying of a string of numbers.

We categorize these various risks as *adversaries*. These are anthropomorphized dangers that each have their own motives for endangering your digital assets. Only by fully understanding them can you determine how to protect yourself against these dangers.

But how do you decide which adversaries are most likely to impact you? More importantly, how do you get past the very human tendency to misjudge risks — either by overestimating them or underestimating them? Risk modeling offers one way to do so: it's a methodical, somewhat regularized way to look at your actual levels of exposure. Our model does so in a few steps: you will characterize your assets; list your vulnerabilities; assess your vulnerabilities; identify the actual risks; and finally correlate those risks to adversarial write-ups.

This Risk Modeling exercise also includes "Alice's Story", a simple custody situation meant to depict how the exercise can be used in the real world. It's intended as a foundation that will allow you to model your own custody scenario, even if it's more complex.

Section I: Asset Characterization

Step 1: Identify Your Assets

The first step in risk modeling is *asset characterization*, where you identify your assets. These are the items that you want to protect. There is some homogeneity among digital assets, but it's still very helpful to eke out every difference you can think of, as that will inform your thinking about vulnerabilities and their risk levels.

For your **cryptocurrency** itself, you should identify where precisely the money is being held, and you may also wish to identify what sort of cryptocurrency it is.

Asset Examples:

- Bitcoin held at Coinbase
- Bitcoin held in cold storage
- Ethereum held in a paper wallet

But talking about the cryptocurrency being held somewhere is actually an abstraction. The **keys** protecting the cryptocurrency are actually *the* crucial asset. There's just usually not a difference between the two: if your Bitcoin is at Coinbase, that means the keys are at Coinbase; and if your Ethereum is only accessible through a paper wallet, that's because you printed your keys in the wallet.

However, if you use a more robust *cold storage procedure*, you might have redundant copies of your keys in several places. In that case, "Bitcoin held in cold storage" is too general of an asset; you instead need to consider each of your copies of a key as an asset, to correctly assess their risks.

Examples of Assets:

- Seed on Ledger in fireproof home safe
- Key on Cryptosteel in safety deposit box

When thinking about these assets, you should also consider their purpose: whether they're long-term investments or currencies intended for trades. This is a topic you'll return to in Step 9.

Finally, you should consider whether there are other, more non-physical assets that you want to protect. Do you care about **privacy** regarding your identity? Are you concerned about **compartmentalizing** your activities? Do you want to ensure **confidentiality** of your total funds? Is **ease of access** something that you want to protect?

List each asset of value to you, including funds, keys, and non-physical assets that you want to protect.

Alice's Story. *Alice is a Bitcoin investor. Subsequent to its rise to $1,000 in late 2013, she used a Coinbase account to buy at various dips. She invested about $50,000 at prices between $250 and $400 between 2014 and 2016, netting a total of 150 BTC. She stopped investing after the price permanently climbed above $400.*

Though Alice has kept a lot of her funds at Coinbase, she's occasionally moved some of it to paper wallets, based on suggestions that she's read at Bitcoin websites. She felt that level of security was good enough. But then on December 16, 2017, Alice checked her Bitcoin value for the first time in a few months and discovered that her 150 BTC were now worth $2.8 million dollars. Bitcoin has dropped from that height, but Alice's coins are still worth more than a million dollars, and so Alice has realized that she needs to protect them better.

To begin her risk modeling procedure, Alice lists her assets. Besides her Coinbase account, and the cold storage of her paper wallet, Alice is also concerned about her privacy, because she fears that she would be targeted if people knew that she had one or two million dollars in cryptocurrency.

1. *Bitcoins at Coinbase*
2. *Bitcoins in cold storage*
    a. *Paper wallets stored in a file cabinet*
3. *Privacy of cryptocurrency ownership*

Step 2: Value Your Assets

Now that you've identified your assets, you need to value them. Use whatever scale you feel will help you to meaningfully separate valuations, provided that it's something that you can easily represent on a graph (in Step 8). Our examples will use a 10-point scale.

For the **cryptocurrency** itself, these valuations will probably correspond to the value of the funds. Your most valuable cryptocurrency will probably be a "10", but if it's just a fraction of your savings and investments in other places, you might rate it as a "4" or a "5".

The **keys** are a little harder to value. If you only have one key for a specific stash of cryptocurrency, then the valuation is exactly the same (and you probably didn't list them separately). However, if you have multiple encrypted backup keys for a fund, they're individually considerably less valuable because the loss or even theft of one copy of a key is much less likely to endanger the cryptocurrency itself. If you instead have multiple unencrypted backup keys, the valuation is much closer to the value of the cryptocurrency itself — both because they're easier to recover from and because they're more prone to theft.

For **non-physical assets**, consider their value in relation to the digital assets themselves. Is your privacy or the possibility of correlation more or less valuable than your funds? Perhaps it's half as valuable if the asset ultimately protects your funds, but perhaps it's twice as valuable if the asset has a larger meaning in your life, such as privacy that protects your reputation.

Enumerate the value of each of your assets.

Alice's Story. Alice has moved about 100 BTC to paper wallets over the years and has about 50 BTC sitting at Coinbase. That seemed like a reasonable amount of liquidity when bitcoins were valued at $300, but is a lot to keep in a hot wallet now that bitcoins are valued at $8,000.

Alice writes down a value for each of her assets, on a 10-point scale:

1. *Bitcoins at Coinbase [5]*
2. *Bitcoins in cold storage*
    a. *Paper wallets stored in a file cabinet [10]*
3. *Privacy of cryptocurrency ownership [8]*

Alice uses simple math to lay out her valuations. The paper wallets represent the most value, so she puts that at a 10. The Coinbase monies represent half of that, so she marks that a 5. Losing her privacy could lead to attacks on her funds, causing her to lose some or all of them, so Alice marked that as an 8, saying that it's almost as valuable as her main stash of cryptocurrency.

Step 3: Diagram Your Process

Your digital assets face two different categories of risks: one when it's being stored and another when it's on the move. Thus, the next step is to sketch out your cryptocurrency process by translating your assets list into graphical nodes[52], then showing how money transfers among them. This will allow you to more easily identify all of the elements of your process — and thus determine their vulnerabilities.

To diagram your process, draw a simple illustration.

1. *Draw physical assets as nodes (circles).* This should be assets that represent physical cryptocurrency or keys. They show where your cryptocurrency is stored.
    a. If a physical asset has subassets (such as cold storage with multiple copies of keys), draw those subassets as *subnodes* (*smaller circles*) linked to the main node.
2. *Add any forgotten nodes to your diagram that are part of your cryptocurrency process but were not on your physical assets list.* This is where you see if you left anything off your asset listing. These other nodes could be accounts that don't currently contain funds but that you plan to use as part of your process in the future, or they might just be stashes of less valuable cryptocurrency that you neglected.
3. *Add alternate nodes (dotted circles) for physical assets that aren't cryptocurrency or where the cryptocurrency doesn't belong to you.* These indicate your transferring cryptocurrency to another owner or exchanging it to or from a fiat currency account. They represent going outside of the cryptocurrency arena that you control (and thus outside of the risks you are modeling).
4. *Draw interfaces (arrows) between the nodes.* They show how cryptocurrency transfers from one node to another. Each interface should go in just one direction, so you might have up to two interfaces for each pair of nodes.
5. *Draw non-physical assets as reminders (squares).* They won't link to anything, but are here to keep all of your assets in one (graphical) place.

Examples of Nodes:

- Bank of America bank account (fiat currency)
- Cold storage (cryptocurrency)
- Coinsquare (cryptocurrency)

Examples of Interfaces:

- Exchanging fiat currency for cryptocurrency
- Moving cryptocurrency to an exchange
- Making a cryptocurrency payment

---

[52]A graph is made up of nodes (which are points or vertexes) and edges (which are links or lines). The nodes in your graph shouldn't be confused with Bitcoin nodes. They're just places where you keep your cryptocurrency or other digital assets.

- Sending change back from a cryptocurrency payment
- Moving cryptocurrency to cold storage
- Exchanging cryptocurrency for fiat currency

🔑 **Draw a diagram that translates your assets into nodes and that shows the interfaces where cryptocurrency moves between nodes. Label the nodes and interfaces.**

If you drew nodes that weren't on your asset list, consider if they should be added to it. You don't need to worry about the alternate nodes like fiat currency accounts and payment addresses (which are both beyond the scope of your cryptocurrency risk modeling), but if you found cryptocurrency accounts that you'd neglected earlier, you should definitely add those (and value them).

🔑 **Update your asset lists and valuations with any forgotten nodes, per Steps 1 + 2.**

Alice's Story. Based on her asset list, Alice initially draws two nodes: her cold storage and her Coinbase account. She adds in the paper wallet as a subasset of her cold storage. There's just one interface, an arrow from the hot wallet to the cold storage, for when she freezes funds.

However, Alice quickly realizes that she's neglected some interfaces. if Bitcoin ever gets back to its previous high, Alice may want to sell it all, to retire to the Bahamas. This requires two new interfaces: an arrow back from the paper wallets to Coinbase, then a loopback at Coinbase to allow her to sell her cryptocurrency.

Next, Alice needs to add in alternative nodes that represent endpoints that go beyond what she controls in the cryptocurrency world. To start with, she adds a node for any payees and with it two more interfaces: an arrow from the hot wallet to the payees, then an arrow from the hot wallet back to itself for change. Finally, she adds a node for her Citbank fiat currency account (which has branches in the Bahamas!) and creates an interface for moving her funds to her bank account.

Finally, Alice adds in privacy, which is a non-physical asset.

Whew! Alice thought she had a simple, drama-free setup, but her final diagram of two cryptocurrency nodes, one subnode, two alternate nodes, six interfaces, and one reminder is somewhat complex:

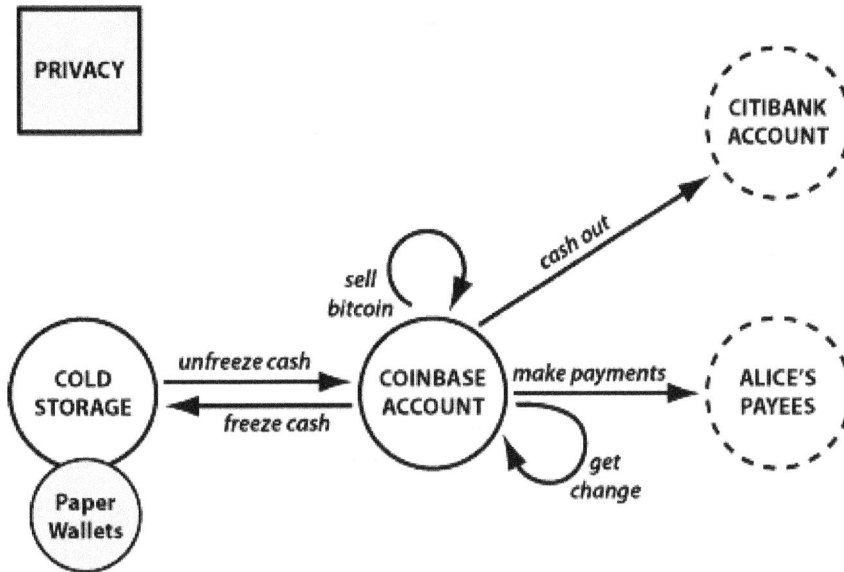

Alice didn't add any nodes, so she doesn't need to update her asset list.

In the meantime, she's happy that she diagrammed out her whole procedure, because it shows how important that Coinbase account is, which makes her a little leary. But that's a problem for the future. For now, she's just seeing what her cryptocurrency setup looks like, and what risks it has. Coinbase as a single-point-of-failure (SPOF) in her diagram is clearly one of them.

Section II: Risk Characterization

Step 4: Brainstorm Interface Vulnerabilities

Now that you've fully characterized your assets, by identifying, valuing, and diagramming them, you're ready to move on to the next step, where you characterize the risks that could affect your assets.

You'll do so by brainstorming *vulnerabilities*, which could cause problems in your digital-asset maintenance, especially those that could eventually lead to the loss of funds. To help your brainstorming you should also consider *threats*, which are active entities who might exploit these vulnerabilities, and *hazards*, which are environmental factors that could exploit these vulnerabilities.

You'll start with vulnerabilities that could impact your interfaces: the places where cryptocurrency moves from one type of custody to another. Write those interfaces down on a piece of paper, then brainstorm about each one individually: what are the vulnerabilities, threats, or hazards that could cause you to lose your cryptocurrency when it moves across that interface?

Be sure that you are truly thinking about *interface* vulnerabilities that occur when cryptocurrency is *moving*, not nodal custody vulnerabilities. The latter will be the subject of Step 5.

Examples of Interface Vulnerabilities:

- Money sent to wrong address
- Incorrect amount of money sent to recipient
- Money lost by recipient
- Money stolen by man-in-the-middle (threat)
- Transaction scripted or timelocked wrong

Creating as thorough of a list as you can on your own, so that you can identify things specific to your setup, will give you a solid start, but afterward please feel free to look at Step 11 for more ideas.

Try to be thorough, but don't go crazy. If something is laughably unlikely, then don't worry about it, but try to walk right up to that line.

> **Make a numbered list of your interfaces, and for each brainstorm a lettered list of reasonable vulnerabilities. Consult Step 11 for additional possibilities when your brainstorm is finished.**

Alice's Story. Alice numbers her six interfaces, then lists possible ways funds could get lost in each of them:

Interface Vulnerabilities:

1. *Freeze cash*

    a. *Paper wallet software did not generate a legitimate address*

    b. *I did not print paper wallet right*

    c. *I did not send to my paper wallet address*

2. *Unfreeze cash*

    a. *I did not send to my Coinbase account*

    b. *Coinbase did not record my transaction*

3. *Make payments*

    a. *I paid to wrong address*

    b. *I paid to spoofed address*

4. *Get change*

    a. *I set change amount wrong*

5. *Sell Bitcoin*

    a. *Purchaser reverses charge*

6. *Cash out*

    a. *Citibank did not record my transfer*

Step 5: Brainstorm Custody Vulnerabilities

You're now ready to move on to your list of nodes, where your funds are held in custody by someone. You can follow a similar process here, where you list your nodes on a piece of paper and brainstorm the dangers of each: how could you lose your funds to vulnerabilities, threats, and hazards while they are sitting on that node? If one of your nodes has subassets, you probably want to brainstorm about the subassets, not the category, as that will more specifically identify the real-world vulnerabilities (e.g., brainstorm about your Ledger wallet, not your cold storage generally).

Don't worry about alternative nodes, like fiat currency accounts, as they're out-of-scope for this cryptocurrency risk modeling.

Examples of Nodal Vulnerabilities:

- Funds stolen by computer attacker (threat)
- Keys stolen by computer attacker (threat)
- Keys stolen in physical theft (threat)
- Keys destroyed in fire or earthquake (hazard)
- PIN for hardware wallet forgotten
- Exchange goes out of business

You might find that multiple nodes have identical vulnerabilities. If so, copy your list of vulnerabilities from one asset to another, but you should still keep them separate: though they have similar vulnerabilities, the likelihood of those vulnerabilities and the consequences might be different, resulting in different risk assessments (see Step 7).

Again, refer to Step 11 for more ideas of risks, after you've created an initial list.

> Continue your numbered list by adding physical nodes, and for each brainstorm a lettered list of reasonable vulnerabilities. Consult Step 11 for additional possibilities when your brainstorm is finished.

Alice's Story: *Alice continues her list by detailing the vulnerabilities that she sees for her Coinbase account and her paper wallets. Though she was somewhat concerned with Coinbase as a single point of failure, when Alice writes out her vulnerabilities, she realizes that the paper wallets are extremely vulnerable too!*

7. *Cold Storage Paper Wallet*
    a. *Paper wallet is water damaged*
    b. *Paper wallet is burnt up in fire*
    c. *Paper wallet is thrown out as junk*
    d. *Paper wallet is stolen by robber*
    e. *Paper wallet is not understood by heirs*
8. *Coinbase Account*
    a. *Company is targeted by hackers*
    b. *Bitcoins are stolen by employee*

Step 6: Brainstorm Non-Physical Vulnerabilities

Finally, you should look at any non-physical assets that you recorded, such as privacy, compartmentalization, and ease of use, and for each of them, brainstorm vulnerabilities for those assets.

Examples of Non-Physical Asset Vulnerabilities:

- Privacy lost due to address reuse
- Privacy lost by announcing Bitcoin ownership
- Ease of use lost by complicated cold storage setup
- Ease of use lost by 2FA
- Compartmentalization lost by constantly sending funds from one account to another

Once more, when you're done with an initial list you might wish to consult Step 11 for additional ideas.

Continue your numbered list by adding non-physical assets, and for each brainstorm a lettered list of reasonable vulnerabilities. Consult Step 11 for additional possibilities when your brainstorm is finished.

Alice's Story: Alice is a little itchy about the interface between her hot wallet and her cold storage. Though she has a couple of different paper wallets, she has reused some of her paper wallets multiple times, when she continued to add bitcoins to them. She also moved funds back to Coinbase a few times in the past, when she thought she was going to sell. This has created potential correlation between her different cold wallets and her Coinbase account. It might be possible to figure out what her total funds are.

Worse, she's used the hot wallet to make purchases a few times — purchases that were shipped to her house under her name. This might allow people to correlate her real name and all of her Bitcoin funds!

This all relates to Alice's non-physical privacy asset, so she writes these problems down as vulneraibilities in her setup:

9. *Privacy*
    a. *Poor address hygiene could correlate cold and hot wallets*
    b. *Purchases from hot wallet could correlate name and Bitcoin assets*

Step 7: Assess Consequences & Likelihoods of Vulnerabilities

One of the most common mistakes in risk modeling is addressing *vulnerabilities* rather than addressing actual *risks.* The whole rigamarole of taking off your shoes and throwing out your liquids at airport security is a modern-day example of protecting against vulnerabilities (the possibility of bombs in shoes or being able to mix an explosive from liquid precursors) without actually assessing their risks (is a shoe bomb likely to work? is it likely to bring down a plane? Is a bomber going to be able to mix up a liquid explosive within the confines of an airplane?) Similarly, the vulnerabilities that you've identified to date for your digital-asset holdings may or may not be realistically exploitable and may or may not have large repercussions.

To turn a vulnerability into a risk requires a simple formula:

risk = vulnerability consequence x vulnerability likelihood

You will now begin the process of transforming the 20 or 30 potential vulnerabilities that you've identified into risks by enumerating a consequence and likelihood for each. And if you're worried about the number of vulnerabilities you're currently dealing with, don't be, because this will be the first step in whittling that long list down into a shorter list of *final* risks.

For each vulnerability, enumerate a consequence and a likelihood:

Consequence is the bad result if the vulnerability proves true, listed as a numerical value. This should be directly based on your asset valuation, from Step 2. If you would entirely lose an asset if a vulnerability proves true, then the consequence value is the same as the asset valuation. If you would lose half of it, then the consequence value is probably half of the asset valuation. The consequence values should be pretty easy to assess, because you already have those asset valuations.

Likelihood is the chance that the vulnerability proves true. Obviously, any assessment of likelihood is going to be subjective: it's going to be based on your gut and whatever level of understanding you have of the cryptocurrency industry. But, by separating likelihoods into ones that *feel* particular unlikely and that *feel* particularly likely, you'll be assessing vulnerabilities in a robust and meaningful way.

Generally, if you can separate likelihoods into *five* levels, that should provide enough differentiation for you to later create a useful chart of risks. Use whatever five categories you would like. They could be letter grades, numbered priorities, or words that are mean something to you.

Examples of Likelihood Measures:

- A, B, C, D, F
- 1, 2, 3, 4, 5
- 25%, 20%, 15%, 10%, 5%
- Constant Problem, Frequent Problem, Occasional Problem, Rare Problem, Extremely Rare Problem
- Very Likely, Somewhat Likely, Possible, Unlikely, Very Unlikely [53]

---

[53]This is the set of terms we use in our examples.

- Almost Certain, Probable, Even, Probably Not, Almost Certainly not [54]
- Super Scary, Cold Chill, Frightening, Concerned, Not Worried
- Great, Very Good, Good, OK, Poor

Use whatever method works best for you; the object is to clearly differentiate different vulnerabilities. Don't worry if you use a different scale than your consequences: you can still lay them out neatly as two axes of a chart (see Step 8).

Try your best to be impartial about these likelihood calculations, which you can do by thinking about them independently from your individual cryptocurrency assets. Comparing the various vulnerabilities will probably help. You could also choose a trusted friend to help you determine likelihoods.

Also, consider adding time into the equation: if an asset is only rarely sitting in a certain wallet, or if an interface is only infrequently used, then the likelihood of a vulnerability being exploited is probably lowered.

Examples of Nodal Vulnerability Likelihood Assessment:

- Funds stolen by computer attacker [occasional problem]
- Keys stolen by computer attacker [occasional problem]
- Keys stolen in physical theft [rare problem]
- Keys destroyed in fire or earthquake [extremely rare problem]
- PIN for hardware wallet forgotten [constant problem]
- Custodian goes out of business [rare problem]

List a consequence and likelihood value for each of your vulnerabilities.

Alice's Story. Alice is now ready to sit down and figure out the consequences and likelihoods of all the vulnerabilities that she's brainstormed. She's going to use five ranked likelihood words: very likely (VL), likely (L), possible (P), unlikely (U), very unlikely (VU).

She starts with her "freeze cash" interface, where she's moving funds into cold storage. She never moves much money at once, so she figures the consequences are low, and she actually thinks that programmatic problems are very unlikely (VU), but ups the odds to just unlikely (U) when she could be the one making the mistake.

Things look a little more scary on the "unfreeze cash" interface, because that's likely to occur when she wants to retire to the Bahamas, so the consequence would be the loss of all her money. Even though she still thinks the likelihood of programmatic errors are very unlikely, the consequences are very high. These assessments recur in the "sell bitcoin" and "cash out" interfaces.

---

[54]These are the "Words of Estimative Probability". We don't use them because none of the risk-modeling odds are likely to be anywhere close to "even"; the vulnerabilities should all be much lower likely events. But, if these call out to you, definitely use them.

The last interfaces are for "make payments" and "get change". Alice thinks there are real opportunities for loss here, but she never makes big purchases, so the consequences are once more low.

Now, Alice moves on to her nodes. Here, she just matches her consequences to the value of the asset. For her two large stores of cryptocurrency, this means that the consequences could be quite bad; when that's matched with high likelihoods, that's a problem.

One thing that Alice notes is that it's a little hard to think about her Coinbase account, because she's currently using it for hot-wallet storage, but someday will use it for selling off all her funds. It might be best not to use the same node for these very different functions, which would also reduce Coinbase as a single point of failure, but again that's an issue for the future. For now she rates her consequences based on what's currently in the nodes.

Alice finishes up with the privacy issues, which could genuinely cause problems due to her casual address hygiene to date.

1. *Freeze cash*
   a. *Paper wallet software did not generate a legitimate address [C: 1, L: VU]*
   b. *I did not print paper wallet right [C: 2, L: U]*
   c. *I did not send to my paper wallet address [C: 1, L: VU]*
2. *Unfreeze cash*
   a. *I did not send to my Coinbase account [C: 10, L: VU]*
   b. *Coinbase did not record my transaction [C: 10, L: VU]*
3. *Make payments*
   a. *I paid to wrong address [C: 1, L: VU]*
   b. *I paid to spoofed address [C: 1, L: P]*
4. *Get change*
   a. *I set change amount wrong [C: 1, L: U]*
5. *Sell Bitcoin*
   a. *Purchaser reverses charge [C: 10, L: SL]*
6. *Cash out*
   a. *Citibank did not record my transfer [C: 10, L: VU]*
7. *Cold Storage Paper Wallet*
   a. *Paper wallet is water damaged [C: 10, L: U]*
   b. *Paper wallet is burnt up in fire [C: 10, L: U]*
   c. *Paper wallet is thrown out as junk [C: 10, L: P]*
   d. *Paper wallet is stolen by robber [C: 10, L: VU]*
   e. *Paper wallet is not understood by heirs [C: 10, L: SL]*
8. *Coinbase Account*
   a. *Company is targeted by hackers [C: 5, L: VL]*
   b. *Bitcoins are stolen by employee [C: 5, L: U]*
9. *Privacy*
   a. *Poor address hygiene could correlate cold and hot wallets [C: 8, L: P]*
   b. *Purchases from hot wallet could correlate name and Bitcoin assets [C: 8, L: P]*

Alice knows that some of these likelihoods might not be entirely right. Listing them all out and considering them comparatively helps her to think about them more dispassionately, but she figures that she still may be overestimating some likelihoods and underestimating others. If she wanted to be really thorough, she'd talk odds over with someone else, and perhaps she'll do that at some time in the future. But for now, this is a good first cut.

Step 8: Chart Consequences & Likelihoods to Reveal Risks

By now, you might already have a rough idea of which vulnerabilities are actually risks that you need to watch out for. However, you can make a more robust analysis by graphing everything in a chart[55].

1. *Label the horizontal axis.* Use your consequences as the horizontal axis, running from 0 to the top consequence that *you considered.*
2. *Label the vertical axis.* Use your likelihood as the vertical axis, running from 0 to the top likelihood that *you considered.*
   a. **Ranked Likelihoods.** If you used ranked words for your likeilhoods, just lay them out in order, with the biggest likelihood being at the top of the axis and the smallest being the closest to the origin (for example: F, D, C, B, A, along the vertical axis).
3. *Place all vulnerabilities on the chart.* Make a point for each vulnerability at the intersection of its consequence and likelihood. Label the point with the letter and number for the vulnerability (e.g., 9A).
4. *Draw a risk-tolerance line.* Finally, you're going to lay out the risk-tolerance line that identifies those vulnerabilities that you should be paying attention to. It will run from part way along the vertical axis to part way along the horizontal axis, creating a triangle of non-risks below it and an open space of actual risks above it.
   a. Figuring out this risk-tolerance line is very individual and will relate to your own level of risk tolerance, so there's no set rule for how to lay it out, but rather a general methodology that you can use to adjust it until you're comfortable with it.
   b. *Evaluate an initial line.* Use a straightedge to lay a potential risk-tolerance line across your graph. Run it from about 70% of the way up your vertical axis to about 70% of the way along your horizontal axis. Take a look at what's on the line or above it and what's below the line and think about how that fits your feeling about risks.
      • **Ranked Likelihoods.** For five ranked likelihood words, 70% will be halfway between the second and third most likely words.
   c. *Generally adjust your line.* If you feel that your risk tolerance is higher, push the straight edge up to 80% or 90% on each side; if you feel that your risk tolerance is lower, push the straight edge down to 60% or 50% on each side.
      • **Ranked Likelihoods.** For five ranked likelihood words, 80% is your second most likely option and 60% is your third most likely option.
   d. *Independently adjust your line.* Alternatively, consider just adjusting one of the axis. If you are more afraid of unlikely events, push the straightedge down along the vertical axis, and if you are less afraid of unlikely events, push it up. If you are more afraid of losing some of your money, pushing the straight edge back on your horizontal axis, and if you less afraid of losing some of your money, push it forward.

---

[55]Some users of this risk modeling system have preferred to lay everything out in a spreadsheet, and then use that to create a graph (or to otherwise identify the risk). That's certainly a fine alternative if you have the spreadsheet expertise.

e. *Draw a final line.* When you're happy that the line matches your risk tolerance, draw it in.

f. *Consider an alternative risk-tolerance curve.* A alternate method draws an asymptotic curve approaching the 20% point for both axes (or the 15% point for less risk tolerance or the 25% point for more risk tolerance). This does a better job of cutting out low-probability and low-value risks but is harder to draw accurately by hand. If you feel up to it, draw it in, then reassess your risks based on what's above both lines (risks), what's below both (non-risks), and what's in-between (possible risks).

- **Ranked Likelihoods.** For five ranked likelihood words, 20% will be at your fifth and least likely word.

🔑 **Draw a chart of your vulnerabilities based on their consequences and likelihood. Draw a risk-tolerance line across the chart to identify the risks. Optionally, eyeball an asymptotic curve to help triangulate high and low risks.**

Alice's Story. Alice charts out all of her vulnerabilities, based on their consequence and likelihood, then draws the risk-tolerance line at 70% from axis to axis.

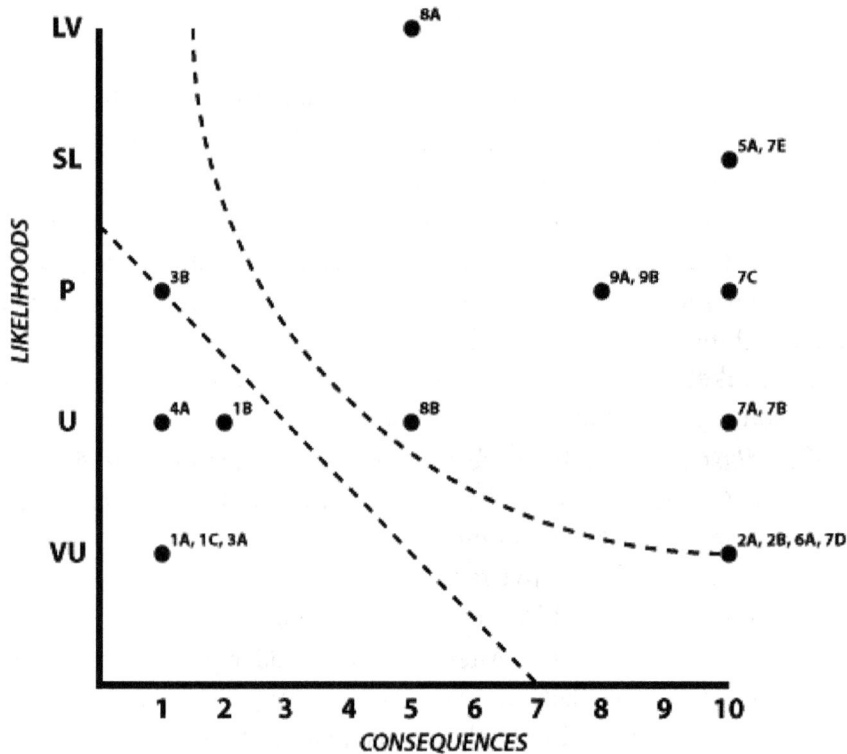

Looking at the chart, Alice is relatively happy with it as a reflection of her-risk tolerance level. It suggests that there's little to worry about when she's freezing small amounts of cash (1), and that when she's making payments, the only thing she should be concerned with is making sure that no one gave her a fake address (3B) — and even that is pretty marginal.

It also highlights where she should have the most concern: the set of interfaces relating to eventually selling off her bitcoins (2: unfreeze cash, 5: sell bitcoin, and 6: cash out); both of her asset stores (8: hot and 7: cold wallets); and her privacy (9).

Alice also draws an asymptotic curve at 20%. Well, it's more of an arc, but it's the best she can easily do. It puts the lower-likelihood risks for her cash out (2A, 2B, 6A, 7D) right on the edge, so she's going to consider them lower risks. It also verifies for her that the spoofed-address payment issue (3B) isn't a big concern because of the small value of her Bitcoin payments.

Step 9: Consider Asset Valuation Changes

So what do you do with risks? Generally, there are four options to resolve them. You've already *accepted* some vulnerabilities by determining that they're low risk or low consequence. There are three other options: *prevention* (where you modify your assets to lower risks), *interdiction* (where you attack the vulnerabilities, threats, or hazards to lower risks), and *mitigation* (where you prepare for the risk by reducing the consequence).

One method of *mitigation* is to modify the valuation of assets to drop them below your risk-tolerance line:

1. *Consider the value of assets.* Look at each of the assets that has a risk, and consider whether their valuation could be decreased sufficiently to push the related nodal risks below the risk-tolerance line. This decision can be influenced by the purpose of the asset.
   a. Generally, it's beneficial to move funds from hot wallets to cold storage. So, for each of your hot wallets, consider if the purpose of some or all of the currency is actually investment, not trading. If so, you should move some or all of the funds.
   b. Even if you can't push an asset below your risk-tolerance line, it can be worthwhile to move it closer to the line, because that's implicitly a reduction in risk
   c. Reducing some risks will inevitably result in increasing others. This is OK. If you're generally happier with the gestalt of the new asset valuations; if the risks better fit the purposes; and if you've shifted risk from hot wallets to cold storage, then you've benefited your overall setup.
   d. Don't bother trying to reduce the valuation of cold storage or those hot wallets where the funds are actually being actively used; you'll instead want to resolve their risks via interdiction, prevention, or different mitigation methods.
2. *Modify consequences.* Based on your asset valuation changes, modify the consequences for those assets, and also consider any linked interfaces and see if their consequences changed as well. (Generally, an interface *originating* with an asset is the one likely to be changed when the asset changes.)
3. *Rechart if needed.* If any valuation changes were made, rechart as per step 8.

This is the first time when you are really examining your procedure for flaws and trying to correct them. You characterized your assets in Steps 1-2 and then you characterized their risks in Steps 3-8. Now you're stepping back and asking if your asset valuations actually make sense.

Examples of Valuation Changes:

- Decide that fewer funds are needed in hot wallet
- Backup keys for cold storage
- Decide that privacy valuation can be reduced by giving some funds to spouse

It could be that you make no changes here, and if you do it's going to be somewhat seat-of-the-pants.

🔑 **Make a plan to move funds that might push risks below the risk-tolerance line or that might replace hot wallets with cold storage.**

Alice's Story. Alice's **hot-wallet related risks** *are the easiest to resolve. There's just no reason to have 50 BTC in her hot wallet, given the current value of bitcoin. So she freezes 40 more BTC. This changes her asset valuation:*

1. *Bitcoins at Coinbase [5̶ 1]*
2. *Bitcoins in cold storage*
    a. *Paper wallets stored in a file cabinet [10]*
3. *Privacy of cryptocurrency ownership [8]*

*This might change the risk analysis for the interfaces originating at the Coinbase node. Most of the Coinbase-originating interfaces already presume very small amounts of money moving, but there was one part of the freeze cash interface that considered a bigger loss; that's now reduced. *

1. *Freeze cash*
    a. *Paper wallet software did not generate a legitimate address [C: 1, L: VU]*
    b. *I did not print paper wallet right [C: 2̶ 1, L: U]*
    c. *I did not send to my paper wallet address [C: 1, L: VU]*

More notably, the Coinbase node itself has dramatically reduced consequences:

8. *Coinbase Account*
    a. *Company is targeted by hackers [C: 5̶ 1, L: VL]*
    b. *Bitcoins are stolen by employee [C: 5̶ 1, L: U]*

*Alice has no idea what do to reduce the **privacy risks**.*

*Finally, she thinks carefully about the **cold-wallet related risks**. Many of them originate from the fact that her paper wallets are all in the same place and they could all be stolen or destroyed in the same way. Spreading out her paper wallets or making additional copies of them would reduce the consequences of fire, flood, robbery, or enthusiastic cleaning, but they'd still be above the risk-tolerance line. Moreso, these are her prime assets, so she wants to prevent the risks, not just mitigate them. So, even though she might be able to reduce her valuations here, she thinks the better answer is carry them forward into the risk resolution section.*

Here's what Alice's new chart looks like, with the changes to her hot wallet valuation:

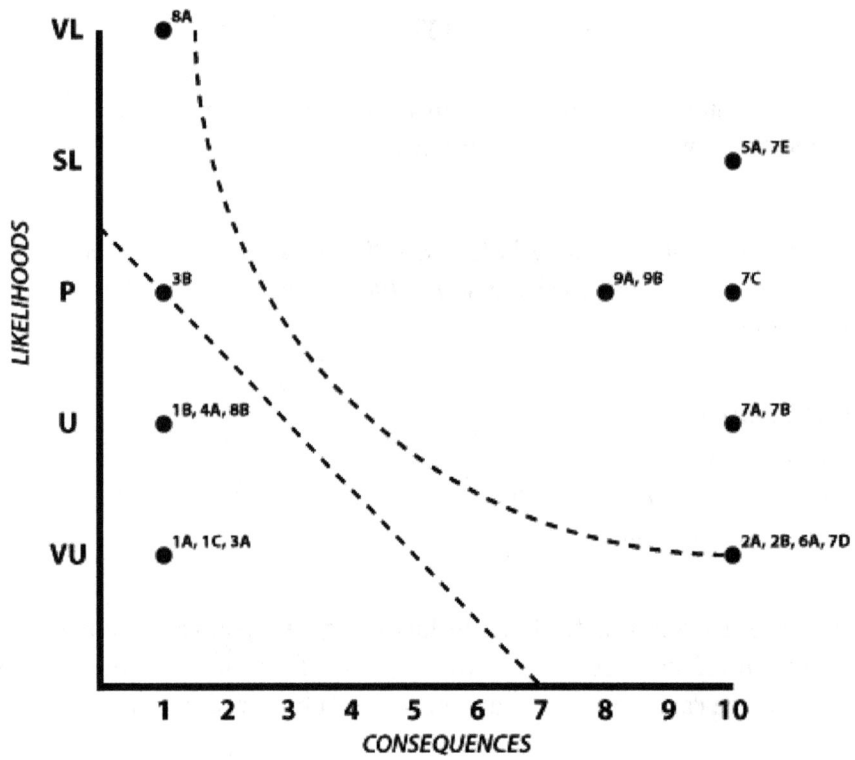

Step 10: List Final Risks

You should now have an updated chart that shows which vulnerabilities are actually risks, because the combination of their consequences and the likelihood exceeds your risk-tolerance threshold. Write out all of the risks that lie clearly above your risk-tolerance line. List them in your best estimation of decreasing order: the further a risk is above your risk-tolerance line, the higher it should go on your list, with the object being to produce a list that has your most notable risks first and your most marginal risks last.

Marginal risks that were on a line or between an asymptotic curve and a straight line may be listed or not, as you see fit.

Use your chart to list risks that lie on or above your risk-tolerance line in decreasing order of risk.

Alice's Story. Alice decides to leave the marginal risks out for the moment, and just lists out the risks that clearly lie above both of her risk-tolerance lines.

1. *5A: Sell Bitcoin: Purchaser reverses charge*
2. *7E: Paper Wallet: Not understood by heirs*
3. *7C: Paper Wallet: Thrown out as junk*
4. *7A: Paper Wallet: Water damaged*
5. *7B: Paper Wallet: Burnt up in fire*
6. *9A: Poor address hygiene could correlate cold and hot wallets*
7. *9B: Purchases from hot wallet could correlate name and Bitcoin assets*

This provides a much more constrained list, which was the point of the exercise. It allows Alice to attack the biggest problems first (and possibly return to others at a later date).

Section III: Risk Resolution

Step 11: Correlate Final Risks to Digital Adversaries

At this point, you might want to immediately start brainstorming ways to interdict, prevent, and further mitigate your risks. If you're knowledgeable about smart custody, and feel like you already know how to reduce your risks, then jump forward to Step 12. However, we have another methodology that may (once more) allow you to approach your risk modeling in a *methodical* way.

What follows is a list of adversaries drawn from the **Chapter Three: Adversaries**. These are sort of like risks, but each of them is an anthropomorphized adversarial entity that contains many related risks, and which details many related solutions. We believe that considering an anthropomorphized adversary of this sort makes it easier to consider the "motives" that might affect you, and also makes it easier to find solutions that address your risks. It's our prime deviation from standard risk modeling methodologies.

Go through the adversary list and checkmark all adversaries that correlate with the risks you identified. Your exact risk might not be here, so try and pick the adversaries that have risks that seem the closest to what you wrote.

The ultimate object here is to take the general, off-the-cuff risks that you identified and to turn them into more abstract, general adversaries, which will help you identify general solutions to these problems.

Examples of Digital Asset Adversaries

1. *Adversary: Bitrot — a hardware, software, or media failure leading to loss*
   - Entropy causes software to stop running, as computer is upgraded.
   - Entropy kills computer.
   - Entropy kills hardware.
   - Entropy kills hardware wallet.
   - Entropy makes Bitcoin keys (or seeds) obsolete.
2. *Adversary: Blackmail — threat of exposure*
   - Attacker sends ransom note to demand bitcoins.
   - Attacker uses Ransomware to demand bitcoins.
3. *Adversary: Censorship — network denial that prevents the use of funds*
   - Attacker blocks site from creating transactions.
   - Attacker blocks you from creating transactions.
4. *Adversary: Coercion — threat of death, disability, or detention*
   - Attacker kidnaps you.
   - Attacker threatens you.
   - Attacker kidnaps your family, friends, or pets.
   - Attacker threatens your family, friends, or pets.

5. *Adversary: Convenience — decreased security due to ease of use*
   - You reduce security, enabling attacks.
   - You grant privileges to someone untrustworthy.
6. *Adversary: Correlation — a connection of funds based on their usage*
   - Analyst connects your Bitcoin addresses.
   - Analyst connects your real address to Bitcoin funds.
7. *Adversary: Death / Incapacitation — a mortal loss or disability that could endanger funds*
   - Heirs can't access cryptocurrency.
   - Heirs don't know about cryptocurrency.
8. *Adversary: Denial of Access — physical denial that prevents use of funds*
   - You can't access physical location of funds.
   - You can't move freely.
9. *Adversary: Disaster — a sudden, large-scale destructive event*
   - Bomb destroys keys or makes them inaccessible.
   - Earthquake destroys keys or makes them inaccessible.
   - Fire destroys keys or makes them inaccessible.
   - Flood destroys keys or makes them inaccessible.
   - Other natural disaster destroys keys or makes them inaccessible.
   - Warfare destroys keys or makes them inaccessible.
10. *Adversary: Institutional Theft — a theft by a trusted institution or its employee*
    - Employee backdoors system.
    - Employee secretly copies keys.
    - Employee steals keys.
    - Institution falsely claims they never received payment.
    - Institution steals everything & disappears.
11. *Adversary: Internal Theft — a theft by a trusted person such as an heir or executor*
    - Hacker tricks trustee.
    - Trustee loses key.
    - Trustee refuses to multi-sign.
    - Trustee steals keys.
12. *Adversary: Key Fragility — an accidental key loss*
    - Someone throws out your keys.
    - System incorrectly generates keys.
    - You lose your encryption method for keys.
    - You lose your PIN.
    - You miscopy your keys.
    - You misplace your keys.
13. *Adversary: Legal Forfeiture — a legal civic or state seizure of funds*
    - Court seizes funds.

- Federal agent seizes funds.
- IRS seizes funds.

14. *Adversary: Loss of Fungibility — a blacklisting of funds based on their provenance*
    - Analyst discovers Bitcoin previously used by undesirable entity.
    - Analyst discovers Bitcoin previously used for illegal activity.

15. *Adversary: Nation-State Actor — wide-ranging threats related to surveillance and coercion*
    - Federal agents steal funds.
    - Federal laws threaten funds.
    - State surveils usages of funds.

16. *Adversary: Network Attack, Personal — a personal online attack*
    - Attacker breaks into account holding private keys.
    - Attacker steals private key for Bitcoin.
    - Attacker steals password or other credential to Bitcoin account.

17. *Adversary: Network Attack, Systemic — *a server online attack **
    - Attacker steals from exchange.
    - Bankruptcy occurs at online company.
    - Keys become unavailable due to exchange disappearance.

18. *Adversary: Non-Financially Motivated Attackers — an attack not intended to steal funds*
    - Attacker breaks things for fun.
    - Attacker steals funds to give away.
    - Malware destroys keys.
    - Spyware correlates fund usage.

19. *Adversary: Physical Theft, Casual — an opportunistic physical theft*
    - Thief steals computer, smartphone, or other key-holding device.
    - Thief accidentally steals keys.

20. *Adversary: Physical Theft, Sophisticated — a purposeful physical theft of private keys*
    - Thief purposefully steals keys.
    - Thief tricks you into handing over keys.

21. *Adversary: Process Fatigue — errors caused by the complexity of the overall procedure*
    - You lose funds while perfecting your procedure.
    - You lose keys while checking keys.
    - You overly obfuscate your keys.

22. *Adversary: Social Engineering — a social theft*
    - Attacker creates fake recipient address.
    - Attacker phishes Bitcoin user.
    - Attacker tricks Bitcoin user into installing malware

23. *Adversary: Supply-Chain Attack — a logistical theft*
    - Attacker modifies computer before purchase.
    - Attacker modifies hardware wallet before purchase.
    - Attacker modifies USB stick before purchase.

24. *Adversary: Systemic Key Compromise — a key-generation compromise*
    - System generates addresses incorrectly.
    - System generates keys insecurely.
25. *Adversary: Terrorist / Mob — a potentially mortal threat related to coercion*
    - Attacker kidnaps you — and death is likely.
    - Attacker threatens you — and threats are real.
    - Attacker kidnaps your family, friends, or pets — and death is likely.
    - Attacker threatens your family, friends, or pets — and threats are real.
26. *Adversary: Transaction Error — incorrect transaction details leading to loss*
    - You create an invalid smart contract.
    - You copy the wrong address.
    - You miscalculate the change amount and send too much to miners.
    - You send the wrong amount of funds.
    - You send to the wrong address.
    - You timelock your funds incorrectly.
27. *Adversary: User Error — an operator mistake leading to loss*
    - You don't maintain your key location.
    - You forget your key location.

That's a big list, but the object isn't to thoroughly understand all of these adversaries, but instead to convert your ideas about vulnerabilities into our standard adversary profiles. And if some of them are scary, that probably means that you should be thinking about them (and hopefully avoiding them).

After you've selected your adversaries, your should write them out in a list of decreasing problems. This might match precisely with your risk list, but some adversaries might get bumped up because they correlated to several risks that you identified. Keep the references to your asset and interface numbers, so that you can reference them later.

🔑 **Convert your risks to a list of adversaries.**

Alice's Story. Reading through the list of adversaries, Alice links each of her risks to something from the adversary list:

1. *5A: Sell Bitcoin: Purchaser reverses charge — **Social Engineering***
2. *7E: Paper Wallet: Not understood by heirs — **Death / Incapacitation***
3. *7C: Paper Wallet: Thrown out as junk — **Key Fragility***
4. *7A: Paper Wallet: Water damaged — **Disaster***
5. *7B: Paper Wallet: Burnt up in fire — **Disaster***
6. *9A: Poor address hygiene could correlate cold and hot wallets — **Correlation***

7. *9B: Purchases from hot wallet could correlate name and Bitcoin assets — **Correlation***

Most of these were pretty obvious, but Alice has a bit of trouble figuring out how to classify somewone reversing credit card charges after getting her Bitcoin (#1). She finally decided it was an "social engineering", since it feels like another sort of confidence-man attack.

She then organizes her adversaries into an ordered list, so she knows how to prioritize them. She uses her order from the true risks, but moves disaster up above key fragility since it's linked to two different problems:

1. *Social Engineering [5A]*
2. *Death / Incapacitation [7E]*
3. *Disaster [7A, 7B]*
4. *Key Fragility [7C]*
5. *Correlation [9A, 9B]*

She's now ready to figure out what to do about these problems!

Step 12: Take Steps to Foil Adversaries

Once you've identified the adversaries most relevant to you, you need to determine how to foil them. To begin, read the *Chapter Two* more closely for the problems that you've recorded through this process. Browse through the entire write-up for each of those adversaries, to better understand the adversary and its relationship to your particular procedure. Pay special attention to the sections at the end: the list of Process, Hot Wallet, and Cold Storage Solutions.

Once you've read through the adversaries and understood them, you should adopt solutions as appropriate:

1. *Introduce a Cold Storage Procedure.* If you already have a cold-storage procedure, you should update it with our *Cold Storage Procedure.* If you don't have a cold-storage procedure, you should consider introducing one, especially if some of your adversaries suggest doing so.
2. *Incorporate Cold Storage Solutions.* Many potential solutions deal generally with the general procedures for cold storage, suggesting how to make it less prone to failure. Consider these and adopt them as required.
3. *Add Cold Storage Optional Steps.* There may also be specific and precise optional steps that can be added to your cold-storage procedure. These steps can be simply integrated into our standard *Cold Storage Procedure.*
4. *Incorporate Hot Wallet Solutions.* Hot Wallet Solutions suggest procedural updates that will keep online funds safer (though online funds are always in greater danger). Consider incorporating them for any hot wallet sites that you have identified as being in danger. Also consider one more time if you can move assets from hot wallets to cold storage (or if you can move them from a more vulnerable hot wallet to a less vulnerable one).
5. *Incorporate Process Solutions.* Finally, some adversaries will require more general process solutions, where you'll need to make changes to your overall way of doing things. This is especially true for interface risks and non-physical asset risks, but it can also apply to general cryptocurrency storage processes. These are the most extensive solutions listed in the Adversaries document.

You will probably *not* choose to use all of the Solutions for your Adversaries, but at least consider each in turn. Then, choose a reasonable subset to work on for your first cut. Don't overdo it, or you could end up losing the ability to do *anything*. Instead, use the best or most important. Pay attention to solutions related to your highly ranked adversaries or that show up more than once. Maybe you'll return to the rest at some time in the future.

> **For each of your adversaries, adapt solutions for cold storage, for hot wallets, and for your processes.**

Alice's Story. Alice reads through her five adversaries, and creates an extensive list of possible solutions.

Process Solutions:

1. Maintain Emergency Procedure.
2. Practice Anonymity. **(x2)**
3. Practice Anonymizing Your Funds.
4. Practice Key Hygiene.
5. Proactively Visit Sites.
6. Redundantly Relay Your Secrets. **(x2)**
7. Register Your Funds.
8. Reveal Your Funds.
9. Take the Time. **(x2)**
10. Use Funds Multisignatures.
11. Verify Your Keys.

The process solutions are full of good advice, but there's more than Alice can deal with at one time. So, she focuses on the ones that either show up multiple times or else are closely related. She's going to work at being better with anonymity (#2) by creating new IDs to talk about Bitcoin that don't correlate to her real identity. And, because it's closely related, she's going to improve her key hygiene and never reuse an address again (#4). Finally, she's going tell her husband, Oscar, about all of her funds (#8), which is closely related to making sure he has the secrets necessary to access them (#6). She writes the rest of the possible solutions in a notebook for future consideration.

Cold Storage Solutions:

1. Fortify Your Key Storage.
2. Redundantly Store Your Keys. **(x3)**
3. Widely Separate Your Keys.
4. **Cold Storage Scenario** *Optional Steps:*
   a. Hire a Lawyer
   b. Use Bags (Fire-Resistant)
   c. Use Metal Enhancement (Redundant Metal Devices) **(x2)**
   d. Use a (USB) Laser Printer

Alice clearly needs to improve her cold storage procedure, especially since she moved more funds there. The key takeaway seems to be that she needs to redundantly store her keys, probably in a safety deposit box, and that she should use something more durable than her paper wallets.

After working through the Cold Storage Scenario she applies most of the optional steps suggested. She ends up with a Ledger in a fire resistant bag in a fireproof safe at home, a second Ledger in a safety deposit box, and a trio of CryptoTags divided between her home safe, her safety deposit box, and her lawyer. Though she lives in the San Francisco East Bay, she rents a safety deposit box down in San Jose, to fulfill the key separation that's suggested. They're not exactly widely separated, but they're on slightly different earthquake fault lines, and they're about 55 miles away, which makes it less likely that one natural disaster will hit both. And yet, they're close enough that she won't introduce Process Fatigue: she can just check in with her new bank when she visits friends and family down in San Jose, which she does a couple of times a year.

Alice doesn't see any new hot wallet solutions and she's still pretty unhappy about the exposure of her hot-wallet funds and the problems she's discovered about Coinbase being a single point of failure in her model and about it being used for both spending money and (in the future) selling off her Bitcoin.

Alice thinks carefully about the advice, "Only keep keys on an exchange or brokerage for the minimum amount of time required to make a transaction." She finally decides that she's technically competent enough that she can handle her own hot wallet, which will limit the threat of Personal Network Attacks. So, she moves her funds to a new Electrum wallet. In the future, she'll only use her Coinbase account when she wants to sell off her funds, which should dramatically minimize that exposure.

Section IV: Process Repetition

Step 13: Repeat the Process

And you're done! For now.

Risk modeling is a continuous process, as your assets, valuations, and procedures *will* change over time. But that's especially true after your first trip through this process. In Step 12, you probably made changes to your procedure and maybe to the setup of your hot wallet and your cold storage. This means that your procedure no longer looks like it did at the start of this process!

But, you've done your job for the moment. Take a rest and be confident that your digital assets are more secure than they used to be. Then, in a few weeks or a few months return, and run through this risk modeling again. After two or three times through this process, your digital asset procedure should become relatively stable. At that point, you can just return to this process every year or two, to see if any changes to your assets need to be reflected in an updated procedure.

> **If you made notable changes to your digital asset procedures, repeat this process in three months or less. If things seem stable, then instead come back in a year or two.**

Alice's Story: Thanks to the adjustments to her cold storage and to the introduction of an Electrum wallet, Alice's digital asset procedure has changed a fair amount:

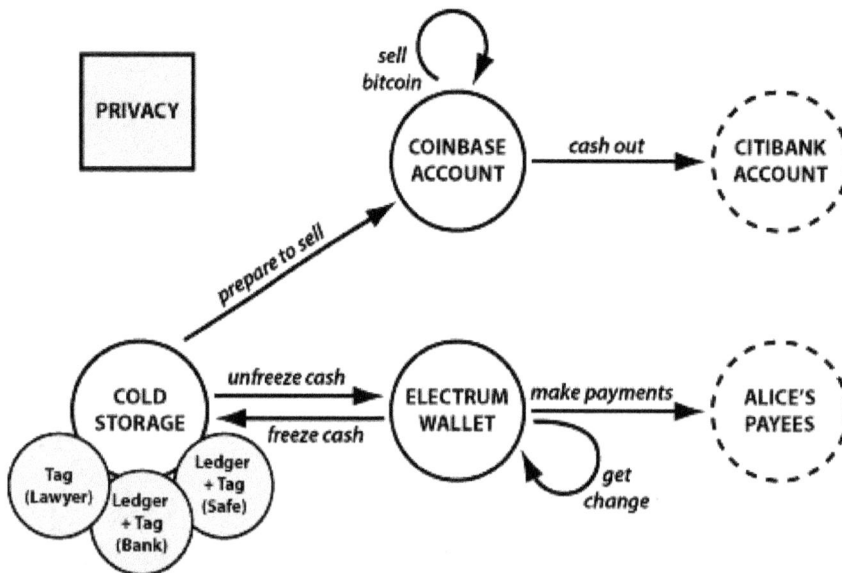

She added a node (the Electrum wallet) and she split up the interfaces coming out of her cold storage, as she could now move funds to her Coinbase account or to her Electrum wallet. (That also cleaned up the problem with Alice's Coinbase account being a single point of failure.) Finally, she added three new subnodes to her cold storage.

Alice's setup has been changed enough that it may now have vulnerabilities that she didn't previously think about. So, she puts a TODO item on her calendar to repeat this exercise in two months.

Other Peoples' Story: For further examples of using this risk modeling methodology see Ilya Evdokimov's "Working with SmartCustody Risk Assessment Framework"[56] on *Medium* and "The Frank Family Fund Example" in **Chapter Five** of this book.

---

[56]https://medium.com/@evdokimov.ilya/working-with-smartcustody-risk-assessment-framework-40ce82538eac

Summary

The object of this risk modeling exercise was threefold.

First, you were taken through a process (Steps 1-10) intended to help you identify risks related to your digital assets in as analytical of a way as possible. Human beings are generally awful at identifying risks because emotions get in the way. So we think that sharks or terrorists are existential threats to our everyday lives, but we underestimate actual risks like getting into a car accident. Analyzing things more abstractly hopefully helped you to step back and make a more balanced assessment.

Second, you summarized the adversaries building block, which you'll meet in more depth in **Chapter Three: Adversaries** so that you could cull through a wide collection of solutions and find the ones that would be the most helpful to you (Steps 11-12).

Third, you repeated the process (Step 13), or at least planned to do so in the future. You'll learn something more each time you repeat the exercise, eliminating both false positives (where you identified something as a risk that wasn't) and false negatives (where you missed a crucial vulnerability).

The specifics of this risk modeling exercise aren't important, except as a tool to help you arrive at your desired goal: more secure digital assets. If something doesn't work for you, transform it, adjust it, or remove it. Just be aware of your goal and of that you're trying to get there by taking emotions out of your decision making and by examining extensive lists of possible problems and solutions as a reference.

Part Two: Building Blocks

This book's risk modeling system offers a comprehensive methodology for assessing and resolving vulnerabilities in your digital-asset storage. It takes you through three major stages: asset characterization; risk characterization; and risk resolution. However, it also depends on two further building blocks, which together form the foundation of that risk modeling system.

A **Cold Storage Self-Custody Scenario** is necessary to thoughtfully protect any digital assets that do not need to be kept in a hot wallet. A comprehensive procedure can protect your assets in cold storage, both from attackers and from your own mistakes.

A list of **Adversaries** further details the many vulnerabilities that may exist in your digital-asset-storage system. Lists of case studies, risks, and solutions can all be used to address vulnerabilities that you've identified through risk modeling.

Chapter Two: Cold Storage Self-Custody Scenario

Best practices for protecting Your personal digital assets using cold storage

Version: 2019-06-07 Release 1.0.2

Introduction to the Custody Scenarios

Digital assets are only as safe as the procedures of their custodian. Many digital-asset holders don't practice minimal safety, and this could result in the loss of all of their Bitcoins, Ether, other digital currencies as well as non-fungible digital assets. The following procedures detail simple and practical setups that can be used as the foundation of safer digital-asset management. The base scenario requires just a few hours setup and then a semi-annual check to make sure everything remains secure.

About The Base Scenario

The base scenario presumes an audience with all of the following characteristics:

- A holder with a significant amount of digital assets (>5% of net worth);
  - with full and legal custody of the assets and no fiduciary responsibility to others;
  - and 100% of those assets shared with a spouse, if present, in estate planning.
- A holder who largely holds investments long term, and is not actively trading them.
- A holder who lives in the first world, and thus is less concerned about issues like government attack, kidnapping, or privacy violations.
- A holder who has sufficient computer skills to comfortably install and run apps.

This scenario suggests that a comprehensive cold-storage procedure would be the best practice to maintain and protect this holder's digital assets. Though simple, this scenario is also a foundation for more complex custodial procedures. It introduces many of the basic approaches for managing digital assets, explains their importance, and presents the adversaries that could steal or ruin the holder's digital assets.

This scenario advocates the basic procedure to address nine major types of adversaries, while the optional procedures can help protect against five further adversaries. Additional categories of "Non-Theft Crimes", "Loss by Government" and "Privacy-Related" adversaries are not strongly considered in this scenario. See **Adversaries**.

For simplicity, this document focuses on Bitcoin, but is easily adaptable to other digital assets supported by our suggested hardware wallet.

If you don't meet the description of the holder for this scenario, it will still be useful, but you will have to adapt it for you specific needs. If you are unsure as to whether you should use a cold-storage scenario, please see Why Cold Storage?.

Procedures

The following procedure will help ensure the safety of a simple self-custody cold-storage scenario for managing digital assets. It is important that you initiate it when you have a large block of time: usually at least two hours when you will not be interrupted and when you will not be distracted. You don't want to make mistakes, and to avoid that it's best to do everything in one go.

Be Careful!

General rule: Don't rush and don't take cold storage lightly!

If you make a mistake you could lose your bitcoin today, or you could expose secret data that would allow an attacker to steal your funds months or years into the future.

Here are some of the more tedious steps, and why they're important:

- *Verify Your Recovery Phrase (D).* Double-checking your recovery phrase ensures that you can rebuild access to your digital currency if you ever lose your hardware wallet(s). By doing it after a small test transaction, you're minimizing your potential loss. *15 minutes, but tedious.*
- *Setup Fireproof Key Recovery Phrase (F).* Embedding your recovery phrase in steel or titanium strongly protects you against Disaster, and also gives you a backup for your hardware wallet and paper recovery phrase. However, it takes a long time to stamp 96 letters. *1 hour.* Be sure to also repeat step D for the phrase you saved in your metal-device. *15 minutes, and still tedious.* If you choose the "Cryptosteel" alternative, that will be equally long.

Don't skimp on any of these phases just because they take a while; don't figure that you'll get back to them later. The goal is to ensure that you protect your digital investments from problems *before* you make any real investments.

Adversaries

This process in this basic scenario has been optimized to avoid risks from ten adversaries listed below — simplified by not addressing the risks of all possible adversaries (over 25+). In particular, these adversaries were the ones selected as most likely to impact a self-custodian in the first world. Adversaries related to "Non-Theft Crimes", "Loss by Government" and "Privacy-Related" are not strongly considered in this scenario.

Some additional processes for this scenario are offered as options—but be careful to avoid Process Fatigue.

1. Key Fragility — *an accidental key loss*
2. Transaction Error — *incorrect transaction details leading to loss*
3. User Error — *an operator mistake leading to loss*
4. System Network Attack — *a server online attack*
5. Death / Incapacitation — *a mortal loss or disability that could endanger funds*
6. Disaster — *a sudden, large-scale destructive event*
7. Personal Network Attack — *a personal online attack*
8. Denial of Access — *physical denial that prevents use of funds*
9. Process Fatigue — *errors caused by the complexity of the overall procedure*
10. Physical Theft, Casual — *an opportunistic physical theft*

The most notable of these adversaries may be "Systemic Network Attack", an adversary that is very problematic in hot-wallet scenarios, but largely nullified by removing private keys into cold storage. In many ways, it's the prime adversary overcome by this scenario.

See **Adversaries** for a more extensive list and discussion.

Requirements

The following items are necessary for this procedure, and should be purchased in advance of your setting up this scenario.[57]

- [ ] Small Home Safe (For example: https://www.amazon.com/AmazonBasics-Security-Safe-0-5-Cubic-Feet/dp/B00UG9HB1Q/[58])[59]
- [ ] Safety Deposit Box at Bank or other institution
- [ ] Existing Laptop or Desktop Computer capable of running Ledger Live[60] [61], preferably able to boot from a USB drive
- [ ] 1 Fine-point Permanent Marker (Sharpie https://www.amazon.com/Sharpie-Plastic-Point-Resistant-1742663/[62] or equivalent)
- [ ] 1 Package Waterproof Laser Paper (TerraSlate, made of 1-PET https://www.amazon.com/TerraSlate-Paper-Waterproof-Printer-Sheets/dp/B00NWVGOF4[63] or Rite in the Rain All-Weather Copier Paper, made of coated recyclable wood https://www.amazon.com/Rite-Rain-All-Weather-Copier-8511/dp/B0016H1RYE/[64] or equivalent)
- [ ] 2 Ledger Nano S, Factory sealed, not used https://www.ledgerwallet.com/products/ledger-nano-s[65] or https://www.amazon.com/gp/product/B01J66NF46[66]
- [ ] One CryptoTag https://cryptotag.io/products/cryptotag-starter-kit/[67]
- [ ] 2 USB cables appropriate for connecting your computer's USB ports to the Ledger (offered as set at https://www.ledgerwallet.com/products/ledger-otg-kit[68]

Please see our footnotes on the Ledger[69] and the CryptoTag[70] for discussions of why we choose that hardware over other alternatives.

***Optional Steps** (described later) may require purchases of additional items.*

---

[57]These items should ideally be sent to your work address or to a UPS or FedEx store for pickup, not a home address, so as not to correlate your Bitcoin holdings and your real name.

[58]https://www.amazon.com/AmazonBasics-Security-Safe-0-5-Cubic-Feet/dp/B00UG9HB1Q/

[59]There's a tradeoff in every decision you make in a security scenario. Here, you have a cheap safe that certainly provides some security, but might draw more attention to your valuables. We don't believe in the alternative, security by obscurity, but this does raise the question of whether you should invest more money in a home safe that's harder to open.

[60]https://www.ledger.com/pages/ledger-live

[61]Current requirements are: macOS 10.9 (64-bit), Windows 8 (64-bit) or Linux Ubuntu 16.10.

[62]https://www.amazon.com/Sharpie-Plastic-Point-Resistant-1742663/

[63]https://www.amazon.com/TerraSlate-Paper-Waterproof-Printer-Sheets/dp/B00NWVGOF4

[64]https://www.amazon.com/Rite-Rain-All-Weather-Copier-8511/dp/B0016H1RYE/

[65]https://www.ledgerwallet.com/products/ledger-nano-s

[66]https://www.amazon.com/gp/product/B01J66NF46

[67]https://cryptotag.io/products/cryptotag-starter-kit/

[68]https://www.ledgerwallet.com/products/ledger-otg-kit

[69]We were forced to make a decision between two major hardware wallets: the Ledger and the Trezor. Both are good, mature solutions with well-reviewed code and solid ecosystems. We ultimately selected the Ledger because it stores its private keys on a cryptographic chip. Since we advocate keeping a hardware wallet in a less-secure home safe, this was a requirement, as it offsets the adversary of Casual Physical Theft. There are disadvantages to the Ledger as well: its cryptographic chip is proprietary, thus unlike the Trezor all of its code isn't open source. Thus, our understanding of its security is ultimately somewhat limited. If another hardware wallet were to appear with an open cryptographic private-key store and open-source code, we would recommend that instead. In the current market, however, we believe that the Ledger device is the best for this scenario. You may substitute a Trezor for this scenario as the tradeoffs are somewhat subjective. (There are also other options such as the Coldcard.)

[70]We similarly chose the CryptoTag because we thought it the best option when compared to alternatives like Cryptosteel and engraved tiles: more discussion of this can be found in the Optional Steps section.

Final State

This procedure will secure your Bitcoin private keys by keeping the more sensitive information in a safety deposit box and the less sensitive information in a home safe, as follows:

Home Safe	Safe Deposit Box
Ledger Device #1	Ledger Device #2
	Ledger PIN
	Paper 24-word seed
	CryptoTag 24-word seed
Instructions for heirs and xpub and cold storage addresses	Duplicates of instructions for heirs and xpub and cold storage addresses

The Basic Procedure

Step A: Setup Safes

1. [ ] Install Home Safe[71]
    1. Ideally it should be physically secured by mounting it to floor or wall joists, or even more securely, directly to a foundation.
2. [ ] Order Safe Deposit Box[72]
    1. Recommendations:
        - Associate it with a joint bank account with at least one of your heirs.
        - Have sufficient funds in the joint bank account for several years of bank fees and box fees.
        - Have the safety deposit box be in both person's names.[73]

Step B: Setup Computer [74]

1. *This optional action is omitted in this basic procedure. Enable it with "Use a USB Drive" if you are concerned about Bitrot or Personal Network Attack.*
2. *This optional action is omitted in this basic procedure, but enabled by "Optional Steps" below.*
3. *This optional action is omitted in this basic procedure, but enabled by "Optional Steps" below.*
4. [ ] Install the Ledger Live software for Mac, Windows or Linux https://support.ledger.com/hc/en-us/articles/360006395553[75]
    1. Download It
    2. Install It

Step C: Create Master HD Seed on Ledger [76]

1. [ ] Start Up Ledger Live

---

[71]Note that most home safes do not offer enough Disaster resistance to sufficiently protect your digital assets. At best they are rated to protect paper against fire. The primary goals of a home safe are to store your PIN-protected key on on a redundant Ledger, to help protect against Physical Theft, Casual, and to provide a secondary location to store a redundant PIN-protected Ledger key in case of physical Denial of Access to your safe deposit box.

[72]It could be argued that this Safe Deposit Box should not be in the same town as your home safe. If a earthquake or fire strikes Berkeley, it is not likely to be as bad in San Jose, and vise versa. You will be visiting it at least once a year, so it should not be too inconvenient. If you are near an international border (for instance in Seattle or Vancouver), it can be useful to have your Safe Deposit Box in another country from your residence to assist against Legal Forfeiture. However, it is more important to be sure that both you and your heirs have easy access to it.

[73]Joint names associated with a joint account should make it more difficult for legal physical Denial of Access to box by the heirs, however, the rules for this differ state-by-state. Ideally this account should be in the form of "joint tenancy" and "tenancy by the entirety". You should seek advice of a local lawyer. See http://www.weisslawstl.com/2008/02/16/joint-tenancy-accounts-safe-deposit-boxes-will-substitutes-will-substitute-will

[74]Higher security scenarios will require the initialization of computer devices and keys generated in a room with no windows, all cell phones removed, laptop cameras, microphones, and home security cameras turned off and taped over, and limited internet connectivity (no wifi). A white noise generator can further foil anything you might have missed. This is not required for this base scenario, but is cheap and easy to do.

[75]https://support.ledger.com/hc/en-us/articles/360006395553

[76]One of the most important principles of these procedures is that the Recovery Phrase (which is the Master Private Key Seed for all of your digital assets) is generated on trusted hardware certified for key creation, and from that point the Recovery Phrase or Master Private Key Seed never resides physically on a network-attached computer.

    1. If necessary, verify for your operating system that you want to run this downloaded app

    2. **On Ledger Live (LL:)** Click "Get started"

2. [ ] Upgrade Ledger (if Needed)

    1. Plug Ledger into computer holding down the right button (furthest from the plug).

    2. Watch for the screen to say "Recovery"; hit both buttons, then hit them again, so that "Settings" pops up on the Ledger.

    3. **LL:** Click "Manager"

    4. **LL:** Click "Use an Initialized Device"; choose your Ledger type and hit "Continue".

    5. **LL:** Just click "Yes" on the Security Checklist questions; they're not actually relevant currently.

    6. **LL:** Click "Check Now" on the Ledger Genuine Check.
   - If it stalls out, it's probably because you didn't hit both buttons to get your Ledger to the App screen, which should say "Settings".
   - On your Ledger, right-click to "Allow Ledger Manager" when requested.
   - When it's done, hit "Continue".

    7. **LL:** Choose a password for your Ledger Live software on your computer.

    8. **LL:** Turn off Analytics and Bug Reports on the Bugs and analytics page, to minimize any potential attack surface.

    9. **LL:** Click "Open Ledger Live", then "Got It", then "Open Manager"

    10. At last, you're ready to check the firmware version on your Ledger!

    11. **LL:** If your Ledger does not have the most up-to-date firmware (currently 1.5.5), hit the "Update" button to the right.
   - Follow the instructions you see on screen.
   - Make sure to verify that the identifier matches between your screen and your Ledger, to ensure the security of this update.
   - You may also need to update the MCU. If so, Ledger Live will alert you. You'll need to disconnect the Ledger, then plug it back in while holding the left button this time.
   - You will usually see that the Bootloader is updating, then the MCU, then the Firmware. (Whew!)

    12. Disconnect your Ledger from your computer; exit Ledger Live.

3. [ ] Initialize Your Ledger

    1. Restart Ledger Live; enter your password; and plug your Ledger back into your computer.

    2. Click both buttons on your Ledger when it says "Welcome"; this is generally how you clear a screen.

    3. Click both buttons again.

    4. You should now see "Configure as new device" with an "X" to the left and a "√" on the right. This means that you hit the left button to choose "No" ("X") and the right button to choose "Yes" ("√"). Click the right button.

4. [ ] Create Your PIN[77]

---

[77]Though not supported by Ledger Live today, some other wallet software allows the encryption of the Recovery Phrase with an additional password using BIP38. We recommend in this base scenario AGAINST encrypting the Recovery Phrase. The loss of a password in an encrypted Recovery Phrase is one of THE most common reasons for bitcoin loss. In this procedure the Recovery Phrase is unencrypted in the most secure location and is thus available as last resort.

    1. Hit both buttons on your Ledger to create a PIN

    2. Create at least a 6-to-8 digit PIN

    3. If you desire PIN compatibility with Trezor, don't use the number "0".

    4. Hit both buttons to verify your PIN

    5. [ ] Write the PIN and the Date that the key was generated using permanent marker on waterproof paper page

5. [ ] View Recovery Phrase

    1. Hit both buttons on your Ledger to view your 24-word Recovery Phrase

    2. Afterward, you can hit the right button to go to the next word

6. [ ] Write down Recovery Phrase, adding it to the waterproof paper page

    1. Write it in 6 rows, with 4 words in each row

    2. Beware of homonyms or similar words

    3. Leave some room at the bottom of the page for notes

    4. Afterward, go back through all 24 words, and look at each character in the words to make sure you got them right

        • Never, *never* put your Recovery Phrase on a connected device. If a device is connected to a network, it can be hacked and even a local copy of your Recovery Phrase will be stolen.

    5. Hit both buttons to exit the word list, then hit both buttons to verify your Recovery Phrase

    6. You'll need to verify all 24 words; expect this to take some time.

    7. You should see "Your device is now ready".

7. [ ] Install Bitcoin on your Ledger[78]

    1. **LL:** Choose the "Manager" in Ledger Live

    2. Hit the right button on your Ledger to Give Permissions

    3. **LL:** Install Bitcoin

    4. **LL:** Hit "Close"

    5. **LL:** Repeat for any other cryptocurrency you want to use

8. [ ] Create Your Bitcoin Account

    1. **LL:** Click the "+" next to Accounts to Add Accounts

    2. **LL:** Choose Bitcoin and hit "Continue"

    3. On your Ledger, hit the right button to navigate to the Bitcoin app, then both buttons to run

    4. Click the right button to allow your Ledger Live wallet to access your Ledger

    5. **LL:** Hit "Continue" in Ledger Live

    6. **LL:** Name the account (e.g. "Investment Cold Storage"), select the checkmark, and hit "Add Account"

    7. Hit the "X" button; you're done: you now have an account to send and receive bitcoins; discount the Ledger

9. [ ] Write the date the key was generated, the Ledger firmware version number, and the Bitcoin app version number on waterproof paper.[79]

---

[78]Though we describe here how to install Bitcoin on your Ledger, the Ledger software actually supports multiple cryptocurrencies. The same procedures can be adapted for any other cryptocurrencies that you are holding.

[79]Why? Because if there is ever a systematic attack on the chips (as happened with the Infineon chip in the YubiKey), firmware (as happened with the Trezor), firmware app, or client software, you can know if you were possibly affected.

Step D: Verify Recovery Phrase

1. [ ] Restart Ledger Live, plug in your Ledger Nano, and login to both.
2. [ ] **LL:** Click "Manager", and find "Recovery Check" in the List of Apps. "Install".
3. [ ] Navigate to "Recovery Check" on your Ledger. Hit both buttons to enter it.
4. [ ] Select both buttons on your Ledger to begin the check. Hit both buttons twice more.
5. [ ] Select 24 words with both buttons, then hit both buttons again.
6. [ ] Enter your 24 words, selecting letters one at a time.
    1. The Ledger will only list possible letters.
    2. The Ledger will provide you with complete word possibilities after you enter two to four letters from each word.
    3. When offered word options, hit the right arrow until you get to the correct word.
    4. Select the right word with both buttons, then hit both buttons again to go on to the next word.
7. [ ] If you see "Recovery Phrase Matches", you have verified your phrase!
    1. If you didn't, check for simple mistakes. If you see them, repeat step D.
    2. Otherwise, restart from step C-3.

Step E: Create Test Transaction [80]

1. [ ] Generate a test receive address
    1. **LL:** Select the "Receive" Menu item on Ledger Live
    2. If necessary navigate to the Bitcoin app on your Ledger and open it
    3. **LL:** Click "Confirm" and you'll see a receipt address on your computer screen with a QR code.
    4. You will also see the address on your Ledger; carefully compare all the digits and if it is the same, hit the right button to confirm.
    5. Write down, copy, or scan the Bitcoin address.
    6. If you write it by hand, double check the address: read it aloud as you look at both the original and your copy.
2. [ ] Send yourself a small Bitcoin transaction to that address. Wait for confirmation.
    1. If you instead request a transaction from someone, best practice is to send them the address via two secure communications methods that are out of band with each other (or else: show them a QR code in person).
    2. After sufficient time has elapsed, you should see the transaction in your Bitcoin account on Ledger Live

---

[80]You may be tempted to skip this step. **Don't.** Transmitting cryptocurrency is a somewhat technical, somewhat unforgiving task. As discussed in the Adversaries Chapter, there are numerous ways that errors can be introduced into cryptocurrency transmission, such as accidentally writing down the wrong address or recording a spoofed address. Sending a small amount of cryptocurrency to an address before committing larger amounts will address some of these potential errors and is a critical (if minimal) step to protect your electronic investment. Even after that initial test, you should still be extremely careful every time you send cryptocurrency, to avoid devastating problems like forgetting to return your change to a change address.

3. [ ] OPTIONAL: Use the "Send" menu item in Ledger Live to send some (but not all) of your test funds back to a different Bitcoin wallet. This confirms that your wallet can not only receive bitcoins, but spend them too[81]. Again, wait for confirmation.

4. [ ] Export account info from Ledger Wallet Bitcoin
   1. Select your account (e.g. "Investment Cold Storage")
   2. Click "Edit Account" (the wrench) on the right
   3. Click "Advanced Logs"
   4. Write, copy, or print the xpub and the address path, along with the account name
   5. [ ] OPTIONAL: Write the name of the account, the xpub, and the root path on your waterproof sheet
   6. Repeat for additional accounts.

5. [ ] Once you've confirmed receipt of your transaction, and possibly spent part of it, disconnect the Ledger

Step F: Setup Fireproof Key Recovery Phrase [82]

1. Set up your CryptoTag
   1. [ ] Stamp the the first four letters of each word in your Recovery Phrase into your CryptoTag.
      - Place the Bit Holder over each row before you begin stamping that word.
      - Carefully check each letter before you stamp it, to be sure you haven't grabbed a look-alike letter. Watch for "O" and "Q" in particular, because they look the same and are near to each other.
      - Be sure the word "CryptoTag" is facing you, so that the letter will be face-up.
      - Stamp forcefully to ensure that the stamped letter is distinct and easy to read. You may find that two blows are necessary to get it sharp and distinct; if so, be sure not to move the stamp in between.
      - Consider taking a break after stamping the first 12 words, to keep your stamps strong and deep.
      - The first four letters of each word are sufficient to distinctly identify each word.
      - If you make a mistake during this process which renders the tag unusable (missing or wrong words, wrong order, etc) consider starting over with a new seed; it is difficult to adequately destroy a partially created CryptoTag.
   2. [ ] After completing all 24 words, reclip the CryptoTag.
   3. See: https://cryptotag.io/tutorial/[83] for a video tutorial.

---

[81] Obviously, if you don't spend your test transaction, you'll lose it if you choose to erase your devices and start over with a new Recovery Phrase.

[82] I recommend titanium; as it has a melting point of 3287℃ it will likely survive a disastrous fire. Steel is good, with a melting point of between 1300° - 1500℃ will survive most common fires. Either, combined with fireproof envelope and stored in a bank safe deposit box, should survive most disastrous situations.

[83] https://cryptotag.io/tutorial/

Step G: Verify Recovery Phrase & Software Standards Conformance

1. [ ] Use same PIN and restore Recovery Phrase on second Ledger.
    1. Use the Recovery Phrase from your Cryptosteel, to verify its accuracy.
2. [ ] Connect the Ledger to your computer and run Ledger Live. Verify that the test transaction is listed and confirmed.

Step H: Transfer Existing Cold Funds

1. [ ] Generate new receive addresses and transfer existing cold funds to the new master seed protected by the Ledger. Wait for confirmation.
    1. Have an appropriate amount of paranoia for the amount of funds you're transferring and your own peace of mind.
    2. Never put enough into a single transaction that it would be catastrophic to lose.
    3. Perhaps start transferring small amounts, increasing over the course of several transactions.
    4. Be sure to see actual confirmations from each transfer before transfering again.

Step I: Print Next Cold Storage Address

1. [ ] **LL**: Open Ledger Live and enter password, click "Receive", and hit "Continue" once the right account has been selected.
2. [ ] Plug in your Ledger, enter the PIN, navigate to the Bitcoin app, and hit both buttons to select.
3. [ ] **LL**: Hit "Verify" and double-check the address on your screen against the one on your Leder.
4. [ ] Write on a separate waterproof sheet the new Receive Address.
    1. After you write it, carefully double- and triple-check it.
    2. Look not just for mistakes, but also where your printing might be ambiguous.
    3. If you prefer, scan the QR code.

Step K: Duplicate USB drive

This optional step is omitted in this basic procedure. Enable it with "Use a Second USB Drive" if you are concerned about Bitrot or Key Fragility. You must also have enabled "Use a USB Drive" previously.

Step L: Prepare Instructions for Heirs and/or Executor

1. [ ] Print instructions for Heirs and/or Executor on waterproof paper, with information on bitcoin exchange accounts, spare hot wallets, and other digital assets. See example letter in Appendix I.

Step M: Store in Safes [84]

1. [ ] Sign the plastic case of your Ledgers with a permanent marker, or use an engraving tool to sign it.[85]
2. [ ] OPTIONAL: Store materials in tamper-evident bag and sign it; [ ] OPTIONAL: Store materials in fire resistant bag.
3. [ ] Place encrypted key-related devices and non-key devices in your Home Safe, including one Ledger, the your instructions for heirs, and one copy of the xpub and cold storage addresses. The safe should NOT have a copy of any unencrypted recovery phrases or the PIN.
4. [ ] Place unencrypted key-related materials in the safety deposit box, including the CryptoTag and the paper Recovery Phrase and PIN. Also store duplicates: the second Ledger, the second copy of instructions, and one copy of the xpub and cold storage addresses.

Step N: Check Storage A — Spring [86]

1. [ ] Confirm contents of Home Safe.
2. [ ] OPTIONAL: If using any tamper-evident bags, check for tampering.
3. [ ] Check to see if there have been any exploits against the Ledger hardware, the Ledger firmware, Ledger Live, or your OS. If there are, you may need to recreate your OS drive from scratch before connecting it to the Ledger.
4. *This optional action is omitted in this basic procedure. Enable it with "Use a USB Drive" if you are concerned about Bitrot or Personal Network Attack**.*
5. [ ] Connect your Ledger, open Ledger Live, and confirm balances.
6. [ ] OPTIONAL: Save any transaction logs on waterproof paper and cstore in Home Safe.
7. [ ] OPTIONAL: If you have used your cold storage address, print new set.

Step O: Check Storage B — Fall [87]

1. [ ] Sign in to check contents of safety deposit box[88]. Check safety deposit box signature logs to see if anyone else has signed in.
2. [ ] OPTIONAL: If using any tamper-evident bags, check for tampering.
3. [ ] Check to see if there have been any exploits against the Ledger hardware, the Ledger firmware, Ledger Live, or your OS. If there are, you may need to recreate your OS drive from scratch before connecting it to the Ledger.

---

[84]The safe at home is not required, but is convenient. It's most important that there be at least one additional place, besides the safe deposit box, that is somewhat secure against Physical Theft, Casual and that will also protect you against physical Denial of Access, if you are locked out of your safe deposit box.

[85]Like using tamper-proof bags, there are some questions as to how much security is added by physically signing the cases of the hardware, as any attacker sophisticated enough to create a working fake that functions with your PIN could also duplicate the case. However, it is a low cost and easy thing to do.

[86]I suggest spring and fall for reviews, to avoid winter and summer holiday times. For my spring review, as it is near tax time and April Fool's, I focus on the accounting — I check transactions against my balances on my exchange, consider if I need to balance my portfolio, and in general focus on "foolish" mistakes I may have made.

[87]For my fall review, near Halloween and the Day of the Dead, I focus on updating my instructions to heirs, confirming with my heirs that they know about my digital assets and how to get help if they need it, etc.

[88]It is particularly important that you sign in to your safe deposit box yearly. There have been cases where lack of regular access to a box has been interpreted as it being "abandoned" or "dormant", causing its seizure as "unclaimed property" and sale by the state. This has happened in the states of Georgia and California. See http://abcnews.go.com/GMA/story?id=4832471

4. [ ] OPTIONAL: If you have an extra USB drive in the safety deposit box, take it home and boot from USB drive. Do only essential security updates; open Ledger Wallet and confirm balances.
5. [ ] OPTIONAL: Save any transaction logs on waterproof paper and store in safety deposit box.
6. [ ] OPTIONAL: If you have used your cold storage address, print new set.

Optional Steps

Created Adversary: Process Fatigue

The following optional steps can be added to this procedure to improve its robustness and its security. Each optional step addresses certain adversaries: they might be added if you know those adversaries to be a problem for your personal custody scenario, or if you identify the adversaries through the risk-modeling system outlined in this book. However, beware: adding optional staeps ultimately adds to the Process Fatigue of the entire procedure, so care should be taken to ensure that new steps are both important and understood.

Optional Steps:

- Erase Your Ledger(s) — for Physical Theft, Casual, Physical Theft, Sophisticated
- Hire a Lawyer — for Death / Incapacitation, Denial of Access, Institutional Theft
- Seal Metal Tiles — for Institutional Theft, Internal Theft
- Use Bags (Fire-Resistant) — for Disaster
- Use Bags (Tamper-Evident) — for Institutional Theft, Internal Theft, Physical Theft, Sophisticated
- Use a (USB) Laser Printer — for Key Fragility, Transaction Error, User Error
- Use Metal Alternative (Cryptosteel) — alternative for Disaster, Key Fragility
- Use Metal Alternative (Steel Tile & Engraver) — alternative for Disaster, Key Fragility
- Use Metal Enhancement (Redundant Metal Devices) — for Denial of Access, Disaster, Institutional Theft, Key Fragility
- Use a USB Drive — for Bitrot, Personal Network Attack
- Use a (Second) USB Drive — for Bitrot, Disaster

See **Chapter Three: Adversaries** for a full discussion of adversaries. The following adversaries appear for the first time in this section:

11. Bitrot — *a hardware, software, or media failure leading to loss*
12. Institutional Theft — *a theft by a trusted institution or its employee*
13. Internal Theft — *a theft by a trusted person such as an heir or executor*
14. Physical Theft, Sophisticated — *a purposeful physical theft of private keys*
15. Supply Chain Attack - *a logistical theft*

Optional Step: Erase Your Ledger(s)

Obstructed Adversary: Physical Theft, Casual, Physical Theft, Sophisticated, Supply-Chain Attack

Created Adversary: Disaster, Key Fragility, User Error

Suggested Complements: Use Redundant Metal Tiles

*A Ledger is a risk for digital-asset management, not just because it's an additional avenue through which the private keys can be accessed, but also because it's a signal flag shouting that the owner has Bitcoins. By erasing a Ledger after its initial setup, issues of "**Loss by Crime / Theft**" can thus be reduced. In addition, it somewhat reduces the danger if there was a **Supply-Chain Attack** on your Ledger. For this optional step, the xpub information is usually excluded too, with the theory being that the Ledger and its information can be restored from the keys and used whenever it's needed.*

*The problem, of course, is making sure that the keys aren't lost; reducing the number of places that a key is stored increases the problem of Key Fragility and may also make a procedure more prone to Disaster. So, this step should only be taken by someone who is **very, very** comfortable with the rest of this scenario, and who has also taken additional steps to backup their keys.*

*The **Redundant Metal Tiles** enhancement step is a particularly good complement to this one because it ensures private keys are still redundantly stored, but maintains the same high level of protection introduced through this option by scattering the keys across multiple locations.*

Replace step "M" of your procedure as follows, to erase your Ledger before storage:

M. Store in Safes

1. [ ] Erase each of your Ledgers by entering an incorrect PIN three times to clear the master key from device. You will see "Your device has been reset."
    1. Place your Ledgers wherever you want; they no longer need to be secured.
2. [ ] OPTIONAL: Store materials tamper-resistant bag and sign it; [ ] OPTIONAL: Store in fire resistant bag.
3. [ ] Place non-key devices in your Home Safe, including your instructions for heirs, and one copy of the cold storage addresses. The safe should NOT have a copy of any unencrypted recovery phrases.
4. [ ] Place unencrypted key-related materials in the safety deposit box, including the CryptoTag and the paper Recovery Phrase and PIN. Also store duplicates: the second copy of instructions and one copy of the cold storage addresses.

Replace action #5 of Step "N" of your procedure as follows, to restore your Ledger as part of maintenance:

1. [ ] Connect your Ledger and rebuild it.
    1. Hit both buttons to move through the first two screens.
        - Hit the **LEFT** button to refuse to "Configure as New Device".

- Hit the right button to "Restore Configuration".
- Reenter the same PIN and verify, per step "C-3".

2. [ ] Hit both buttons to "Enter your recovery phrase".
   - Choose to restore "24" words.
   - Enter your Recovery Phrase from the waterproof sheet.
   - Enter letters one at a time, selecting with the left and right arrows, then choosing by hitting both buttons.
   - The Ledger will only list possible letters.
   - The Ledger will provide you with complete word possibilities after you enter two to four letters from each word.
   - When offered word options, hit the right arrow until you get to the correct word.
3. [ ] Hit both buttons when words are finished processing, then hit both buttons to open the Bitcoin app.
4. [ ] **LL:** Open Ledger Live and confirm balances.
5. [ ] Erase Ledger by entering an incorrect PIN three times to clear the master key from device. You will see "Your device has been reset."

Similarly, replace action #4 of Step "O" of your procedure as follows:

1. [ ] OPTIONAL: If you have an extra USB drive in the safety deposit box, take it home and boot from USB drive. Do only essential security updates. Connect your Ledger and rebuild it.
   1. Hit both buttons to move through the first two screens.
      - Hit the *LEFT* button to refuse to "Configure as New Device".
      - Hit the right button to "Restore Configuration".
      - Reenter the same PIN and verify, per step "C-3".
   2. [ ] Hit both buttons to "Enter your recovery phrase".
      - Choose to restore "24" words.
      - Enter your Recovery Phrase from the waterproof sheet.
      - Enter letters one at a time, selecting with the left and right arrows, then choosing by hitting both buttons.
      - The Ledger will only list possible letters.
      - The Ledger will provide you with complete word possibilities after you enter two to four letters from each word.
      - When offered word options, hit the right arrow until you get to the correct word.
   3. [ ] Hit both buttons when words are finished processing, then hit both buttons to open the Bitcoin app.
   4. [ ] **LL:** Open Ledger Live and confirm balances.
   5. [ ] Erase Ledger by entering an incorrect PIN three times to clear the master key from device. You will see "Your device has been reset."

Optional Step: Hire a Lawyer

Obstructed Adversary: Death / Incapacitation, Institutional Theft

Created Adversary: Process Fatigue, Institutional Theft

A lawyer can store sealed files for you and will have a fiduciary responsibility to maintain them safely and privately[89]. This can reduce the problem of Institutional Theft for those concerned about various privacy or legal issues regarding safety deposit boxes, but you obviously must ensure the lawyer is trusted. This option can also increase the odds of your heirs or family accessing your digital assets, because the lawyer will know what to do if Death / Incapacitation occurs. But there is new danger of Process Fatigue, if nothing else because a lawyer is an ongoing cost.

Replace the safety deposit box in action #4 of step "M" and in step "O" with a lawyer; or, alternatively supplement your safety deposit box to also include the same information with a lawyer in a sealed envelope.

---

[89]Before giving any digital asset key material to a lawyer, make sure the materials are sealed in an opaque envelope in a tamper-evident bag. Never tell your lawyer your 24 words over the phone and never ask the lawyer to write down your 24 words.

Optional Step: Seal Metal Tiles

Obstructed Adversary: Institutional Theft, Internal Theft

Created Adversary: Process Fatigue

Metal tiles can be dangerous because they leave cryptographic seeds in plain text. One solution for this problem is to use a sealant to place a unique opaque cover over the words, so that looking at the words would be tamper-evident (because the sealant would have to be removed). For the sealant to be truly tamper-evident, it needs to have a unique cover that you can recognize when you revisit it, so that you know no one has removed it, then recovered it. Glitter is applied over the sealant for this purpose. This can counter Institutional Theft and Internal Theft.

The deficit of sealing your plates in this way is that it'll make the plates very hard to access. That's fine for the emergency when you need to use them to recover your funds, but less so if you want to check them every once in a while, thus there is definite Process Fatigue.

This process is not likely to work equally well for all sorts of metal devices. It's probably better for an ad hoc method, like using an engraver on a metal tile. It might work on CryptoTag, though it's untested. It's definitely not appropriate for something like CryptoSteel.

Add the following actions to Step "F" if you are using one or more CryptoTags or metal tiles:

1. Seal the metal tile with a plastic coating.
2. Use a glitter polish to give the coating a unique finish.
3. Photograph the unique pattern of the glitter finish.
4. Store photograph in alternate location.

In Step "O", when you check your safety deposit box, you should always compare your photograph to the finish on the metal tile.

Add the following to your requirements list:

- Plastic Sealant – https://www.amazon.com/dp/B00I9SK8XY[90]
- Glitter Polish — https://www.amazon.com/essie-luxeffects-nail-polish-stones/dp/B007RS4R9I[91]

---

[90]https://www.amazon.com/dp/B00I9SK8XY
[91]https://www.amazon.com/essie-luxeffects-nail-polish-stones/dp/B007RS4R9I

Optional Step: Use Bags (Fire-Resistant)

Obstructed Adversary: Disaster

Created Adversary: Process Fatigue

Fire-resistant bags can increase the fire resistance of printed materials, and thus protect against Disaster. If used in combination with a fireproof safe, they may add to the rated time. However, note that fire-resistant bags are not specifically designed for protecting electronics: they are intended to protect non-electronic materials. They may not add any additional protections to computers, hardware wallets, USB sticks, or other such devices, and they may not even protect InkJet-printed material. So, don't overly depend on this optional step.

Add the following action to step "M" of your procedure:

1. [ ] Store all materials in fire-resistant bags.

Add the following to your requirements list:

- 2 Fireproof Bags — 11 x 15" https://www.amazon.com/gp/product/B01NCVKZXG[92] or 11 x 7" https://www.amazon.com/gp/product/B01KWTE9ZU[93]

One bag is used for your home safe, one for your safety deposit box.

---

[92]https://www.amazon.com/gp/product/B01NCVKZXG
[93]https://www.amazon.com/gp/product/B01KWTE9ZU

Optional Step: Use Bags (Tamper-Evident)

Obstructed Adversary: Internal Theft, Institutional Theft, Physical Theft, Sophisticated

Created Adversary: Process Fatigue

Tamper-evident bags can be used to reduce Internal Theft, Institutional Theft, and Physical Theft, Sophisticated because it becomes more difficult to surreptitiously look at key material. For paper materials they slightly decrease risk of damage due to water used by firefighters, and thus may help a little in Disaster.

They can also increase Process Fatigue because of the need to replace the bags whenever examining the key material.

Add the following action to step "M" of your procedure:

1. [ ] Store materials in tamper-evident bag, record the serial number, and sign it.

Add the following to your requirements list:

- 2 Opaque Tamper-Evident Deposit Bags https://www.amazon.com/MMF-Industries-2362010N06-12-Inch-Tamper-Evident/dp/B000J05F06[94]

One bag is used for your home safe, one for your safety deposit box.

---

[94]https://www.amazon.com/MMF-Industries-2362010N06-12-Inch-Tamper-Evident/dp/B000J05F06

Optional Step: Use a (USB) Laser Printer

Obstructed Adversary: Key Fragility, Transaction Error, User Error

Created Adversary: Various varieties of Theft.

Printing information from your computer rather than hand copying it can improve Key Fragility and can reduce Transaction Error and User Error. However, be aware that a laser printer might keep what you printed in memory, opening you to Theft. Do not use a printer that will ever be reattached to a network, and clear its memory if you know how.

Add the following action to step "B" of your procedure:

5. [ ] Install printer drivers for USB Printer

Instead of writing, print out your receive bitcoin addresses (I.4), the extended public key (E.7), and anything else from Ledger Live, all on waterproof laser paper.

Add the following to your requirements list:

- USB Laser Printer (do not enable ethernet or wifi)

Optional Step: Use Metal Alternative (Cryptosteel)

Obstructed Adversary: Disaster, Key Fragility

Created Adversary: Physical Theft, Casual, Disaster, or Institutional Theft

Cryptosteel is primarily an alternative to CryptoTag, which means that it can similarly increase protection against Disaster or Key Fragility. The advantage of using Cryptosteel is that it's the most precise of all the metal-device options: you put specific letters into the Cryptosteel case, so there's no opportunity for unreadable text. The disadvantage is that its fiddly and may not be entirely Disaster resistant — it has been reported[95] that in one high-temperature torch test that the Cryptosteel twisted and some of the letters popped out.

As with any unencrypted copy of your master seed, you should protect it somewhere like a safety deposit box, or you'll increase your vulnerability to Physical Theft, Casual. However doing so increases the likelihood of Institutional Theft, so be sure to assess which is more likely given your situation.

This is one of three possible options for maintaining a copy of your Recovery Phrase using a metal-device to increase its durability and Disaster resistance. CryptoTag is our default choice, as we believe it best combines fire resistance [96] and preciseness. Of our two optional choices: Cryptosteel is more precise but more fiddly; while a Metal Tile & Engraver are cheap and simple, but can lead to precision problems with messy transcription.

Replace the first action in step "F" of your procedure; alternatively, add this action to step "F" if you want to use a Cryptosteel in addition to CrypoTag.

1. Set up Cryptosteel
    1. [ ] To open your Cryptosteel, rotate the two sides counter-clockwise.
    2. [ ] To unlock one side of your Cryptosteel, rotate the screw 90 degrees counterclockwise, then push down the pawl in the inset toward the bottom right. Afterward, swing open the locking arm. Be sure you're starting with the "1"-"12" side.
    3. [ ] Set the letter tiles for the first four letters of each word in your Recovery Phrase into the CryptoSteel.
        - Carefully check each letter as you place it, to be sure you have the right side, and you haven't grabbed a look-alike letter.
        - The first four letters of each word are sufficient to distinctly identify each word.
        - Some letters will slide easily, some will need to be pushed with the small screwdriver you used to open your Cryptosteel. Occasionally, you may get one that doesn't fit at all.
        - Lock the arm when you're done, and repeat on the "13"-"24" on the other side.
    4. [ ] After completing all 24 words, on both sides, close the Cryptosteel.

In step "M", store the Cryptosteel in your safety deposit box.

Add the following to your requirements list:

---

[95] https://medium.com/@lopp/metal-bitcoin-seed-storage-stress-test-21f47cf8e6f5
[96] https://twitter.com/crypto_tag/status/1073206843525222400

- Cryptosteel Master Mnemonic https://cryptosteel.com/[97] or https://www.amazon.com/gp/product/B0756P57M8
- Small flathead screwdriver

---

[97]https://cryptosteel.com/
[98]https://www.amazon.com/gp/product/B0756P57M8

Optional Step: Use Metal Alternative (Single Metal Tile & Engraver)

Obstructed Adversary: Disaster, Key Fragility

Created Adversary: Physical Theft, Casual or Institutional Theft

A Metal Tile with an Engraver is primarily an alternative to CryptoTag, which means that it can similarly increase protection against Disaster or Key Fragility. The advantage of using a Engraved Metal Tile is that it's simpler and cheaper; the disadvantage is that it's more prone to User Error, as it can be harder to read the letters. (If you prefer, stamp it by hand[99]. Both Steel and Titanium options are available: be aware that Steel has a slightly lower melting point than Titanium, and beware that some tiles advertised as steel are actually aluminum, which has an even lower melting point. (Read the fine print!) Of course, having a engraved tile in addition to the high-end CryptoTag can increase protection even more.

As with any unencrypted copy of your master seed, you should protect it somewhere like a safety deposit box, or you'll increase your vulnerability to Physical Theft, Casual. However doing so increases the likelihood of Institutional Theft, so be sure to assess which is more likely given your situation.

This is one of three possible options for maintaining a copy of your Recovery Phrase using a metal-device to increase its durability and Disaster resistance. CryptoTag is our default choice, as we believe it best combines fire resistance[100] and preciseness. Of our two optional choices: Cryptosteel is more precise but more fiddly; while a Metal Tile & Engraver are cheap and simple, but can lead to precision problems with messy transcription.

Replace the first action in step "F" of your procedure; alternatively, add this action to step "F" if you want to use a metal tile & engraver in addition to CrypoTag.

1. Use Steel or Titanium Tile & Engraving Pen:
    1. [ ] Engrave the 24 word Recovery Phrase on metal plate (recommend 4 rows of 6 tiles)
        - Write in ALL CAPS for clarity.
        - Separate words with "/"s or some other mark.
        - Push hard enough to make a solid, readable mark, but not quite hard enough to stop the engraving pen's motor.
        - It can be very challenging to write clearly with an engraving pen. You'll get better with practice. If something isn't clear, cross-out and repeat.
        - You are only required to write the first four letters of each word to recover, but you may wish to write the entire words for improved clarity.

In step "M", store the metal tile in your safety deposit box.

Add one of the following metal tiles to your requirements list:

---

[99]https://stampingblanks.com/Stamp-Sets/
[100]https://twitter.com/crypto_tag/status/1073206843525222400

- Design Ideas Identity Plate https://shop.designideas.net/product/identitycase-holder-give-taketake[101] or(
- ColdTi Titanium Tile https://www.amazon.com/TopHat-Technologies-ColdTi-Cryptocurrency-Storage/dp/B077CYKHZ6[102]

AND add one of the following engravers to your requirements list:

- Manual scribe https://www.amazon.com/gp/product/B06XYZVJJ6[103] or
- Battery-powered engraver https://www.amazon.com/gp/product/B075Z2QR1[104] or
- Dremel Industrial Engraver https://www.amazon.com/Dremel-290-05-120-Volt-Industrial-Engraver/dp/B000 with Dremel Diamond Tip https://www.amazon.com/Dremel-9929-Engraver-Diamond-Point/dp/B00004UDJ

---

[101]https://shop.designideas.net/product/identitycase-holder-give-taketake
[102]https://www.amazon.com/TopHat-Technologies-ColdTi-Cryptocurrency-Storage/dp/B077CYKHZ6
[103]https://www.amazon.com/gp/product/B06XYZVJJ6
[104]https://www.amazon.com/gp/product/B075Z2QR1
[105]https://www.amazon.com/Dremel-290-05-120-Volt-Industrial-Engraver/dp/B000VZIGA0/
[106]https://www.amazon.com/Dremel-9929-Engraver-Diamond-Point/dp/B00004UDJU

Optional Step: Use Metal Enhancement (Redundant Metal Devices)

Obstructed Adversary: Disaster, Institutional Theft, Key Fragility

Created Adversary: Death / Incapacitation, Process Fatigue, User Error

*Cryptosteel, CryptoTag, and engravable steel or titanium tiles are great for preventing disastrous loss of your key, but introduce a real danger since you're forced to leave an unencrypted copy of your master seed in plain sight. An alternative is to use any of these methods to create a redundant set of three metal-protected copies of your master seed, where each copy contains only two-thirds of your words, and any two copies can recover your seed completely. This continues to protect you from Disaster and Key Fragility but also introduces robust but imperfect[107] protections against **Loss by Crime / Theft**, primarily focusing on Institutional Theft (since you'd usually be protecting your unencrypted master seed in a safety deposit box).*

*The downside of using a two-of-three metal tile strategy is that it introduces complexity into your procedure. When you set up your tiles, User Error could leave you with an incomplete set of 24 words, if you don't break them up correctly. Later, having to constantly collect two out of three tiles can introduce Process Fatigue. Finally, the complexity of this setup might increase the danger of **Danger/Incapacitation** resulting in your digital fortunes being lost.*

Enhance step "F" of your procedure as follows

- Divide the 24 recovery words among the three metal tiles or Cryptosteel devices, placing sixteen words on each, such that any two tiles gives you all of the words.
  1. [ ] Engrave, stamp, or set recovery words 1-16 on the first metal device.
  2. [ ] Engrave, stamp, or set recovery words 1-8 and 17-24 on the second metal device.
  3. [ ] Engrave, stamp, or set recovery words 9-24 on the third metal device.
- If you're etching or stamping a tile, be sure to number your words or place them in the appropriately numbered spaces, so that you know their proper order

Replace the entirety of step "G" of your procedure:

1. [ ] **Test Metal Devices A & B**. Use the same PIN to initiate your second Ledger. Rebuild the recovery phrase from devices A & B, to verify their accuracy and your ability to rebuild the complete Recovery Phrase from them.
   1. [ ] Connect the Ledger to your computer and run Ledger Live. Verify that the test transaction is listed and confirmed.
   2. [ ] Disconnect and reconnect the second Ledger and enter an incorrect PIN three times to clear the master key from device. You will see "Your device has been reset."

---

[107] Note that there is some danger if an adversary accesses one of your three metal-devices. Whereas the 24 words gives you 256 bits of entropy, if an adversary knew 16 words but not the remaining 8, you'd drop down to 80 bits of entropy. This is still relatively safe given the state of modern computers, but is far below the recommended entropy for protecting cryptocurrency long-term. If you lost one of your three metal devices, you should immediately reset your master seed and transfer your currency.

2. [ ] **Test Metal Devices B & C.** Use the same PIN *again* to initiate your second Ledger. This time, rebuild the recovery phrase from devices B & C, to verify their accuracy and your ability to rebuild the complete Recovery Phrase from them.

    1. [ ] Connect the Ledger to your computer and run Ledger Live. Verify that the test transaction is listed and confirmed.

    2. [ ] Disconnect and reconnect the second Ledger and enter an incorrect PIN three times to clear the master key from device. You will see "Your device has been reset."

3. [ ] **Test Metal Devices A & C.** Use the same PIN *one more time* to initiate your second Ledger. This time, rebuild the recovery phrase from devices A & C, to verify their accuracy and your ability to rebuild the complete Recovery Phrase from them.

    1. [ ] Connect the Ledger to your computer and run Ledger Live. Verify that the test transaction is listed and confirmed.

    2. Don't reset it again! Now that you've tested all the combinations of your metal tiles, this is your backup Ledger.

In step "M", store one of the metal devices in your home safe and one in your safety deposit box. The third tile should be placed somewhere else reasonably secure. If you Hire a Lawyer, that's a great location. Alternatively, consider something like a work safe or a safe at your parents' house

In step "N" and "O", pick up the third device at the alternative location, then check it in conjunction with the tile stored at the locale that you are checking.

Add the following to your requirements list:

- TWO extra Steel or Titanium Tiles; or TWO extra Cryptosteels; or TWO extra CryptoTags.

Optional Step: Use a USB Drive[108]

Obstructed Adversary: Bitrot, Personal Network Attack, Supply-Chain Attack

Created Adversary: Process Fatigue, User Error

Your main computer is constantly being updated, and it's quite possible that are some point it'll be updated to a version that no longer works with your cryptocurrency software. This is particularly dangerous when you're using open-source software whose maintenance has degenerated or proprietary software whose company has disappeared. To offset the danger of Bitrot, you can preserve the operating system that you use for cryptocurrency work on a USB Drive, and boot from it whenever you plan to send or receive money. This can also offset some Personal Network Attack dangers, because your cryptocurrency OS will be used infrequently, shielding you from malware. Similarly, it can somewhat reduce the likelihood of a supply-chain attack, if you're using an OS you installed on a USB, as opposed to the one that came with the computer.

The downside of using a USB Drive is that it requires both a fair amount of work to setup and more technical sophistication on the part of the holder than the base scenario: expect at least an hour of additional time, with a somewhat advanced procedure. And, it's a bit of a pain to have to boot it up everytime you want to do anything with your digital assets. These elements can add Process Fatigue and User Error.

Add the following to Step "B":

1. [ ] Create a new bootable operating system on a USB Memory Stick (or USB hard drive)
    1. Format the external USB device
    2. Download the installer for your OS
    3. Install the OS to the external USB drive
2. [ ] Boot drive from USB (This will be very slow! It is ok.)[109]
    1. Many newer operating systems, including MacOS and Windows, disable booting from an external device by default for security reasons. You'll need to flip a security switch to allow it. If you have this issue, your computer should give you a clear message about what to do when you try to boot.
3. [ ] Update with all security updates, but no optional updates and no apps

In step "M", store the USB Drive in your home safe.

Add the following to Step "N":

1. [ ] Boot from USB drive from your Home Safe; do only essential security updates

Add the following to your requirements list:

---

[108]This USB drive is mostly for convenience, to assist against the form of Bitrot that is upgrade rot and to protect against some forms of active attack. The USB drive never has any key material on it, but it does allow you to return to a known working state without adding new code to the system. If a USB drive dies, it can be replaced.

[109]In my case, I confirmed that the USB drive booted on multiple Macintosh models, not just my primary laptop.

- 1 USB Drive (a new, unopened Memory Stick, rated for fastest speed you can find, that will work with your laptop). I like this dual A & C USB Memory Stick https://www.amazon.com/Patriot-Stellar-C-Type-C-Flash-PIF64GSTRCOTG/dp/B015OYNHY2[110] or just a small USB Hard Drive.

More sophisticated users might prefer a read-only USB[111] or a PIN-protected USB[112], though these tend to require more careful use and a clear understanding of when writing is required. They're also somewhat more expensive.

---

[110]https://www.amazon.com/Patriot-Stellar-C-Type-C-Flash-PIF64GSTRCOTG/dp/B015OYNHY2
[111]https://www.amazon.com/FlashBlu30-Physical-Protect-Switch-SuperSpeed/dp/B00JJIEE4M/
[112]https://www.amazon.com/Apricorn-Hardware-Encrypted-Validated-ASK3Z-128GB/dp/B0711KDGML/

Optional Step: Use a (Second) USB Drive

Obstructed Adversary: Bitrot, Disaster, Systemic Network Attack

If you already "Use a USB Drive", you may want to double-up with a second copy. Any usage of a secondary electronic device can protect against Bitrot: since you'll be updating your first USB drive in spring and this second USB drive in fall, if a problem arises with an upgrade, you'll still have a clean copy of the OS on your other drive. Similarly, if a operating system is compromised by Systemic Network Attack, you have a backup.

Add the following step "K" to your procedure:

K. Duplicate USB drive

1. [ ] Reboot computer, and image copy first USB drive to to second USB drive (e.g., with Carbon Copy Cloner)
2. [ ] Confirm that both boot.

In step "M", store the second USB Drive in your safety deposit box.

Add the following to your requirements list:

- 1 (more) USB Memory Stick (new, unopened, rated for fastest speed you can find, and will work with your laptop). I like this dual A & C USB Memory Stick https://www.amazon.com/Patriot-Stellar-C-Type-C-Flash-PIF64GSTRCOTG/dp/B015OYNHY2[113] or 1 (more) small USB Hard Drives.

---

[113]https://www.amazon.com/Patriot-Stellar-C-Type-C-Flash-PIF64GSTRCOTG/dp/B015OYNHY2

Alternative Scenarios

The base scenario suggests a secure way to maintain your digital assets in cold storage. A number of optional steps are all available to you in order to increase your security. Following are some ways in which you may combine those optional steps to serve specific needs.

- Avoiding Private Key Loss
  * Hire a Lawyer, Use Bags (Fire-Resistant, Tamper-Evident), Use a USB Drive, Use a (Second) USB Drive
- Avoiding Private Key Theft, Level 1
  * Hire a Lawyer, Use Bags (Tamper-Evident)
- Avoiding Private Key Theft, Level 2
  * Erase Your Ledger, Hire a Lawyer, Use Bags (Tamper-Evident), Use Metal Enhancement (Redundant Metal Tiles)

Alternative: Avoiding Private Key Loss

Optional Steps: Hire a Lawyer, Use Bags (Fire-Resistant), Use Bags (Tamper-Evident), Use a USB Drive, Use a (Second) USB Drive

Who Should Use This: People afraid that they will lose their digital assets due to misadventure.

If you're afraid that the base scenario doesn't protect you against accidental loss of a key, you may be right: that's probably the most likely way to lose your digital assets, particularly due to Disaster or simple Key Fragility. To avoid that, you can incorporate a few of the optional steps that all relate to increasing your redundancy, with the understanding that they also tend to increase your vulnerability to various types of purposeful "**Loss by Crime / Theft**".

Home Safe	Safety Deposit Box	Lawyer
Ledger Device #1	Ledger Device #2	
USB Drive (OS) #1	USB Drive (OS) #2	
	Ledger PIN	Ledger PIN
	CryptoTag 24-word seed	
	Paper 24-word seed	Paper 24-word seed
Instructions for heirs and xpub and cold storage addresses	Duplicates of instructions for heirs and xpub and cold storage addresses	Duplicates of instructions for heirs and xpub and cold storage addresses
All in a fire-resistant bag	All in a fire-resistant bag	All in a tamper-evident bag, itself in a fire-resistant bag

Alternative: Avoiding Private Key Theft, Level 1

Optional Steps: Hire a Lawyer, Use Bags (Tamper-Evident)

Who Should Use This: People with *some* fear of key theft and little need to trade coins.

If you don't think the base scenario sufficiently protects your unencrypted keys, a few steps can notably increase your security about **Theft**, mainly by taking banks out of the equation. This has some detrimental effects on your accessibility, but they're relatively minor.

Home Safe	Lawyer
Ledger Device #1	Ledger Device #2
	Ledger PIN
	CryptoTag 24-word seed
	Paper 24-word seed
Instructions for heirs and xpub and cold storage addresses	Duplicates of instructions for heirs and xpub and cold storage addresses
All in a tamper-evident bag	All in a tamper-evident bag

Alternative: Avoiding Private Key Theft, Level 2

Optional Steps: Erase Your Ledger, Hire a Lawyer, Use Bags (Tamper-Evident), Use Metal Enhancement (Redundant Metal Tiles)

Who Should Use This: People with *strong* fear of key theft, a *strong* ability to not lose keys themselves, and no need to trade coins.

The increased protection of Level 1 theft protection might be insufficient if you think you are a prime target of cryptocurrency theft or if you don't feel there is anyone you can trust with potential access to this currency. In this case, you don't want to leave your private key accessible at any location. You keep your Ledger clear when it's not in use and your separate your keys into 2-of-3 sets. In order to somewhat reduce the dangers of Key Fragility and Death / Incapacitation, a lawyer is involved to ensure that someone besides you knows how (and why) to put everything back together.

Home Safe	Safety Deposit Box	Lawyer
Words #1-16 on metal dev.	Words #1-8,17-24 on metal dev.	Words #9-24 on metal dev.
Instructions for heirs and cold storage addresses	Duplicates of instructions for heirs and cold storage addresses	Duplicates of instructions for heirs and cold storage addresses
		All in a tamper-evident bag

Chapter Three: Adversaries

Anthropomorphized risks for digital assets

Version: 2019-06-14 Release 1.0.0

Introduction to Adversaries

When creating a digital-asset management procedure, a user adds steps to the procedure based on his vulnerability to a set of more than twenty *adversaries*: if an adversary seems like a danger to a user, then he should introduce optional steps that foil the adversary and otherwise should implement appropriate solutions. Applicable optional steps are listed for many adversaries, measured against a baseline of a user who protects his coins only with a personal safe and a single Ledger.

The term "adversary" is slightly different from the more common "risk" used in the security business. By anthropomorphizing these threats, we can consider their motivations. This helps a custodian to gain some distance from the scenario by making it less personal and so makes it easier for them to determine which adversaries are actual risks *to them*. For example, a user may fear his government stealing his money. This might be tightly tied up with his self-definition as a libertarian or a white hat. But when he flips the script and instead considers the motives of an anthropomorphized government, he removes himself from the equation and can see that the motive of the government is to stop criminal activity and to collect unpaid taxes; he can then make a more informed decision about whether that adversary's motivations are actually relevant to his situation.

Adversary Listing

Following are extensive descriptions of each adversary, covering their motives, their risks, and their solutions. They are divided into categories which help to organize the *most common* origin of each adversary. Short case studies are included for all adversaries, some of them abstracting potential problems, others referring to historical exploits.

1. **Loss by Acts of God**

a) *Adversary: Death / Incapacitation — a mortal loss or disability that could endanger funds*

b) *Adversary: Denial of Access — physical denial that prevents use of funds*

c) *Adversary: Disaster — a sudden, large-scale destructive event*

2. **Loss by Computer Error**

a) *Adversary: Bitrot — a hardware, software, or media failure leading to loss*

b) *Adversary: Systemic Key Compromise — a key-generation compromise*

3. **Loss by Crime, Theft**

a) *Adversary: Institutional Theft — a theft by a trusted institution or its employee*

b) *Adversary: Internal Theft — a theft by a trusted person such as an heir or executor*

c) *Adversary: Network Attack, Personal — a personal online attack*

d) *Adversary: Network Attack, Systemic — a server online attack*

e) *Adversary: Physical Theft, Casual — an opportunistic physical theft*

f) *Adversary: Physical Theft, Sophisticated — a purposeful physical theft*

g) *Adversary: Social Engineering — a social theft*

h) *Adversary: Supply-Chain Attack — a logistical theft*

4. **Loss by Crime, Other Attacks**

a) *Adversary: Blackmail — threat of exposure*

b) *Adversary: Coercion — threat of death, disability, or detention*

c) *Adversary: Non-Financially Motivated Attackers — an attack not intended to steal funds*

d) *Adversary: Terrorist / Mob — a potentially mortal threat related to coercion*

5. **Loss by Government**

a) *Adversary: Legal Forfeiture — a legal civic or state seizure of funds*

b) *Adversary: Nation-State Actor — wide-ranging threats related to surveillance and coercion*

6. **Loss by Mistakes**

a) *Adversary: Convenience — decreased security due to ease of use*

b) *Adversary: Key Fragility — an accidental key loss*

c) *Adversary: Process Fatigue — errors caused by the complexity of the overall procedure*

d) *Adversary: Transaction Error — incorrect transaction details leading to loss*

e) *Adversary: User Error — an operator mistake leading to loss*

7. **Privacy-related Problems**

a) *Adversary: Censorship — network denial that prevents the use of funds*

b) *Adversary: Correlation — a connection of funds based on their usage*

c) *Adversary: Loss of Fungibility — a blacklisting of funds based on their provenance*

Category: Loss by Acts of God

Origin. Bad luck.

Definition. A loss that wasn't caused by any intelligent attacker. An Act of God is something that just happens. You can't prevent it, you can only make it less likely or insure that it damages you less if it occurs.

Iconic Image. Lightning strikes your computer. When lightning suddenly (and surprisingly) hits your computer, it might destroy your only copy of your private keys. You can make this less likely by storing your computer somewhere that lightning is unlikely to strike, and you can reduce the damage by maintaining additional copies of your private keys, but no matter what, that lightning is coming down!

Ulterior Motive. None. Though all of these adversaries list motivations, there is no intelligent ulterior motive behind an Act of God. No one is trying to steal your Bitcoins or prevent you from accessing them. Forces of nature are just working against you, as they do in a universe founded on the Second Law of Thermodynamics.

Adversary: Death / Incapacitation

Motivation. *"I am your last firing neurons, and I seek to drag everything you ever knew down with you, into the darkness."*

Key Words: *Passive.*

The lack of centralization and the high levels of anonymization for cryptocurrency make it hard to know when someone is holding cryptocurrency. This is usually considered a feature, but in the case of death or incapacitation, an asset holder usually want their heirs or guardians to know about the cryptocurrency, lest it be lost forever.

Abstract Case Study: Suffering a Stroke. Bob, an early bitcoin entrepreneur, suffers a stroke that leaves him considerably mentally impaired. His medical bills quickly pile up. Since he left no information about his bitcoins, his wife Alice is forced to sell their house to pay them.

Historic Case Study: The QuadrigaCX Question. The most famous attack of the grim reaper ever reported upon cryptocurrency is certainly the case of QuadrigaCX, where the company claimed that CEO Gerald Cotten had died suddenly in India and taken with him the passwords that provided the only access to the company's cold storage, worth about $145 million dollars. Certainly, this shows how Death/Incapacitation *could* have a large impact on cryptocurrency, but the actual veracity of the claim remains up in the air, as there was initially some question whether Cotten had actually died, and later it was revealed that $100 million dollars were missing from QuadrigaCX's cold-storage wallets. *Engadget*[114], *CoinDesk*[115].

Historic Case Study: Dying with Deposits. A moderator of a bitcoin discussion group knew that he was dying. He was holding not only his own bitcoin funds, but some for the forum as well. After he passed, the other staff of group spoke with his next of kin, to recover their funds, but the next of kin didn't know about the funds, let alone how to recover them. Some time later, the funds still had not moved, suggesting that they were genuinely lost.

Risks:

1. **Funds Loss.** Because of the high level of anonymization for cryptocurrency, no one is ever going to call up an asset holder's heirs or guardians to tell them about the funds. That means that if the asset holder hasn't notified them themselves, the funds will be lost forever.

---

[114]https://www.engadget.com/2019/03/08/quadrigacx-bitcoin-missing-millions/
[115]https://www.coindesk.com/100-million-short-quadrigacx-audit-cant-account-for-26k-missing-bitcoin

2. **Key Loss.** If the asset holder was too careful in hiding their private keys or even just in the methods of obfuscation or protection that they used, then their heirs or guardians won't be able to access cryptocurrency funds even if they know about them. This could also be an issue in multi-sig scenarios, where one or more holders are killed or incapacitated, and suddenly a solution intended to protect bitcoins becomes a new problem.

Process Solutions:

1. **Register Your Funds.** Register and document your funds fully with your nation-state to maximize legal protections. *Dangers: Legal Forfeiture, Nation-State Actor.*

2. **Redundantly Relay Your Secrets.** Tell someone else the secrets required to unobscure or unprotect your private keys or to access your funds. *Dangers: Internal Theft.*

3. **Reveal Your Funds.** Write a letter to your heirs or guardians and be explicit about the existence of your funds. Include instructions on how to access them. Provide information about the necessary passwords or PINs to unlock the private keys. Safely store this letter with a very trusted person, such as your estate lawyer, or in a very trusted place, such as a safety-deposit box. *Dangers: Internal Theft, Institutional Theft.*

Cold Storage Solutions:

1. **Redundantly Store Your Keys.** Maintain multiple representations of your master keys. Store encrypted keys in local storage and unencrypted keys in more protected storage, such as a safety deposit box. *Dangers: Casual Physical Theft, Institutional Theft.*

2. **Cold Storage Scenario Optional Steps:** Hire a Lawyer.

Adversary: Denial of Access

Motivation. *"I want to control your movements, to keep you from getting to your bank or to your house. As is often the case, I have a deeper motivation, but it probably has nothing to do with your cryptocurrency. Instead, my motives likely relate to an instability in your city, state, or country. I might be a riot, a political insurgency, or a popular uprising."*

Alternative Categories: Crime, Misc.

Key Words: Cold Storage, Physical.

Access to cryptocurrency is usually blocked by censorship, when someone on the internet purposefully obstructs the ability to transact funds. However, that blockage can also take physical form if access to private-key storage locations is prevented. This imagines a fairly large-scale problem that is likely only possible in a politically unstable region.

Abstract Case Study: Blocking by Mistake. Frank is cheap, so he stores his Cryptosteel in his company's safety deposit box, which he has access to. The company goes into bankruptcy, and Judy has its assets frozen. Frank tries to recover his Cryptosteel from the safety deposit box but finds he's denied access … which wouldn't be a problem except for the fact that the dog ate the paper copy of his recovery seed at home.

Risks:

1. **Key Denial.** Much as with Censorship, the user still has theoretical access to his keys, but can't actually get to them.

Process Solutions:

1. **Neutrally Store Your Funds.** Maintain funds or keys outside of the sphere of control of fascist and authoritarian nation-states.

Cold Storage Solutions:

1. **Redundantly Store Your Keys.** Maintain multiple representations of your master keys. Store encrypted keys in local storage and unencrypted keys in more protected storage, such as a safety deposit box. *Dangers: Casual Physical Theft, Institutional Theft.*

2. **Widely Separate Your Keys.** Maintain multiple physical representations of your master keys in places that are widely separated. Consider locales under different legal jurisdictions and with different physical risks.

3. **Cold Storage Scenario Optional Steps:** Hire a Lawyer, Use Metal Enhancement (Redundant Metal Devices).

See Related Adversaries — Censorship.

Adversary: Disaster

Motivation. *"I want to destroy. I want to crumble and burn. I want to ruin with water, to blow things into the air. I am bombs, bullets, and explosions. I am sudden and unexpected but disastrous destruction."*

Key Words: *Cold Storage, Physical.*

A sudden, large-scale destructive event can destroy copies of private keys. It is usually a natural event such as an earthquake, fire, hurricane, or tsunami. It could also be an accident such as a building collapse; or it could be a man-made catastrophe, such as a bomb blast, an EMP blast, or full-scale warfare.

Historic Case Study: Flooding Keys. A bitcoin user had a strong procedure for protecting his keys. Every quarter he reprinted his paper wallet to ensure that the ink didn't fade and immediately shredded the old one. Unfortunately, he placed his paper wallet in the basement, which flooded; the ink was washed off the wallet. The user came to IRC for help, and though they suggested dumping his printer's memory buffer, it was already too late.

Risks:

1. **Key Destruction.** The physical representations of private keys could be lost. Electronic devices could be damaged sufficiently that keys can no longer be recovered. Printed copies of keys could be burned by fire, ruined by water, or destroyed by physical force.

2. **Key Loss.** Even if not destroyed, the physical representation of a key could become unavailable. It might be buried under a destroyed building, lost behind the lines of a war, or washed out to sea.

Cold Storage Solutions:

1. **Fortify Your Key Storage.** Ensure that the physical representations of keys are protected against disaster. Write on waterproof paper or etch on fire-resistant steel or titanium. Use sturdy, fortified hardware devices that are more likely to survive disasters. Use fire-proof bags as an additional level of protection.

2. **Redundantly Store Your Keys.** Maintain multiple representations of your master keys. Store encrypted keys in local storage and unencrypted keys in more protected storage, such as a safety deposit box. *Dangers: Casual Physical Theft, Institutional Theft.*

3. **Widely Separate Your Keys.** Maintain multiple physical representations of your master keys in places that are widely separated. Consider locales under different legal jurisdictions and with different physical risks.

4. **Cold Storage Scenario Optional Steps:** Use Bags (Fire-Resistant); Use Metal Enhancement (Redundant Metal Devices); Use a (Second) USB Drive.

Category: Loss by Computer Error

Origin. Computers & software.

Definition. A loss caused by computer hardware or software. All cryptocurrency depends upon computers, but they can let you down when their hardware or software fails, due to poor production, poor programming, or just poor luck (which would be a Loss by Computer Error caused by Act of God).

Iconic Image. Smoke billowing up from a computer. A dying computer is the most evocative example of computer error, but Loss by Computer Error could be caused by the quieter destruction of aging parts or the simple incompatibility of obsolescence. Similarly, you could have smoke (metaphorically) billowing up from a computer program, which failed to do what it should do due to programmer error.

Ulterior Motive. None. As with an Act of God, no one is explicitly trying to take your funds through Computer Error. There's just bad luck, focused on your computer hardware or software, which makes you unable to access your funds — perhaps, forever!

Adversary: Bitrot

Motivation. *"I am entropy writ large. I want to break down your storage, crash your hard drives and degrade your optical media. I want to prevent your computers from booting, your programs from running, and your data from reading; in the end, I always win."*

Alternative Category: Act of God.

Key Words: Cold Storage, Technological.

Electronic storage methods for private keys can become unusable over time. This could be a physical hardware problem: hard drives can crash or old computers can fail. It could be an issue with electronic storage media: USB flash drives are often cheaply made, while optical media can fail in a relatively short amount of time depending on its specific manufacture. It could be a problem with aging software: a new version of software might have a bug or might not work like old software, a hardware device might have its software fail over time, or a new computer might no longer be able to run an old, required piece of software. It could be a time-related hardware incompatibility: old media may no longer be readable on new devices, or old plugs may not fit into new ports.

Abstract Case Study: Obsoleting Software. Carol loads up her Bitcoin wallet for the first time since she upgraded to Windows 10 ... and discovers that it doesn't run. Digging further, she learns that it's been years since the developer of the wallet updated it. She has no idea of how to recover her keys from the wallet.

Historic Case Study: Obsoleting Seeds. A user on StackExchange reported that he had a 15-word recovery phrase and a passphrase for his Bitcoins, but he had no idea what wallet had generated it. This isn't the standard 24-word phrase used by Ledger or Trezor, nor the variant phrases used by Electrum or GreenAddress. Despite having the codes, he didn't know what to do with them. **StackExchange**[116].

Historic Case Study: Throwing Out Bitcoins. James Howells of the UK is widely reported to have accidentally thrown out the hard drive with keys for 7,500 bitcoins after he broke down his laptop for parts. **News Story**[117].

---

[116]https://bitcoin.stackexchange.com/questions/65171/how-to-restore-wallet-from-15-word-seed-mnemonic
[117]https://www.cnbc.com/2017/12/20/man-lost-127-million-worth-of-bitcoins-and-city-wont-let-him-look.html

Risks:

1. **Key Destruction.** Some of the more disastrous forms of bitrot result in the total annihilation of the key.
2. **Key Loss.** In other cases, the key might still be on the hardware, but if the hardware doesn't boot or if the software doesn't run, it's nonetheless lost.

Cold Storage Solutions:

1. **Backup Your OS File System.** Make a copy of the known-working operating system files that you used on the computer that manages your keys.
2. **Maintain Setup Information.** Record as much information as you can about your computer and wallet setup, so that an expert can help to restore your state. Try to use open-source software and backup the source code. Verify that the source code corresponds to the version of the software that you are using. Also store wallet documentation.
3. **Physically Store Your Keys.** Store a physical representation of a key on a non-electronic medium, such as paper (or steel). *Dangers: Disaster, Casual Physical Theft, Institutional Theft.*
4. **Rotate Your Key Storage.** Move your keys on to newer hardware as it becomes available. *Dangers: Correlation.*
5. **Verify & Rotate your Backups:** Make multiple backups of working operating files that are kept in different locations. Use alternating backups or consider a *"Tower of Hanoi*[118]*"* rotation strategy. Be sure to verify your backups as part of a regular schedule.
6. **Verify Your Key Storage.** Regularly test your key storage to make sure that it's still working. If a key storage method becomes inoperative, quickly replace it.
7. **Cold Storage Scenario Optional Steps:** Use a USB Drive; Use a (Second) USB Drive.

See Related Adversaries — Key Fragility

---

[118]https://en.wikipedia.org/wiki/Backup_rotation_scheme#Tower_of_Hanoi

Adversary: Systemic Key Compromise

Motivation. *"I lie in wait. I want you to think that your keys were generated correctly, but after you've turned your attention to other things, I will spring my surprise. I am the best pal of hackers and crooks, who use my exploits to steal your money."*

Alternative Category: *Mistakes.*

Key Words: *Technological.*

A systemic problem in the generation of keys can leave them broadly vulnerable to compromise. For example, a key-generation program's random seed might have been insufficiently random. This might be a result of an error in the key generation or purposeful malevolence on the part of the key generators. This may also be an attack on a system meant to steal all of the keys on that system or to deny access to it.

Historic Case Study: Whitehatting BlockchainInfo. A mistake in an update caused 0.0002% of Blockchain.info's private keys to be generated insecurely. 250 Bitcoins quickly went missing, but it was soon revealed that a whitehat was sweeping up the funds, with the intention of returning them. **News Story**[119].

Historic Case Study: Trusting Libraries. Systemic compromises can arise from deep libraries used in cryptocurrency apps. JavaScript's secureRandom() function at one time generated low-entropy numbers that weren't truly random due to a type error. Unfortunately, it was used in numerous cryptocurrency products for many years before this was discovered. **Security Alert**[120], **News Story**[121].

---

[119]https://cointelegraph.com/news/white-hat-hacker-returns-missing-bitcoins-to-blockchaininfo
[120]https://lists.linuxfoundation.org/pipermail/bitcoin-dev/2018-April/015873.html
[121]https://btcmanager.com/vulnerability-in-javascript-function-may-mean-long-term-bitcoin-hodlers-are-at-risk/

Risks:

1. **Funds Loss**. A sophisticated attacker could use the compromise to discover private keys. This would most likely occur in aggregate, rather than the asset holder being individually targeted.

2. **Cascade: Censorship**. One of the possible results of a systemic key compromise is the censorship of the system.

Process Solutions:

1. **Maintain Emergency Procedure**. Write a procedure that describes what to do if your security has been compromised. Follow it quickly and precisely. Generally, move funds if their keys have any possibility of compromise. *Dangers: Process Fatigue.*

2. **Monitor the Industry**. Read Bitcoin news sites or use a system like Google Alerts to receive relevant news, so that you can be aware of happenings in the Bitcoin industry, particularly security compromises.

3. **Rotate Your Keys**. Regularly change the keys being used to protect funds by sending those funds on to new addresses. *Dangers: Key Fragility.*

Hot Wallet Solutions:

1. **Question Policies & Procedures**. Know the security policies and procedures of any company that you're working with; be sure that they have rigorous, well-documented security procedures that they follow religiously, and that they treat any variance from their procedure as a problem that must be investigated. Also, be sure that there are no negative policies that might affect your usage of its services.

Category: Loss by Crime, Theft

Origin. Thieves.

Definition. A loss caused by a criminal taking your keys (and thus funds) from you. Explicit theft is what most cryptocurrency holders are worried about, though it might not actually be the most common cause of loss. There can be a number of different sorts of Theft, differing based on who is doing the stealing (an anonymous thief or a trusted friend) and how they're doing the theft (by network, physically, or by a confidence scheme).

Iconic Image. A masked burglar taking keys from a safe. Our iconic image of theft is drawn from heist movies, but more often Theft occurs as a result of a sophisticated network attack where the thief is never anywhere near your physical key storage.

Ulterior Motive. Greed. The thief wants to take your cryptocurrency from you, so that he can have it himself.

Adversary: Institutional Theft

Motivation. *"I pretend to be a good employee, but I'm always waiting for my chance for a great score. I want to sift through the goods entrusted to my company and to take the best for myself. However, I don't want to be caught, so I need to be cautious in my larceny."*

Key Words: *Active.*

Keys could be stolen by the staff members at a trusted institution such as a bank or a Bitcoin exchange. This could be a bank employee violating dual-access-key protocol and illicitly accessing a safety deposit box or it could be an engineer stealing private keys out of a database. Unlike casual or sophisticated theft, the physical representation of the key might not be stolen, just the data, making it harder for the victim to realize that a theft has occurred at all!

In rare cases, a whole institution might be corrupt. They might steal the coins or some of their customers, they might falsely claim that a hacker had made off with funds, or they might just disappear quietly, never to be heard from again.

Abstract Case Study: Backdooring the System. Mallory always plans for the future. While working at an exchange as their security expert he builds several backdoors into the system. Years later, when the value of bitcoin has skyrocketed, he utilizes them, and the exchange finds their funds suddenly missing.

Historic Case Study: Blocking Hackers. Sometimes an Internal Theft might actually be a purposeful choice on the part of a company to retrieve stolen goods! When coins were stolen from the OzCoin mining consortium they were moved to a StrongCoin Wallet. This was obvious due to a correlation danger at StrongCoin: every time funds are spent at StrongCoin, a small fee is paid to a specific address. OzCoin alerted StrongCoin who recovered the funds by creating a new version of their JavaScript wallet especially for the hackers; as soon as they tried to access the funds, the coins were sent to another address, so that StrongCoin could then return them to OzCoin. **News Story**[122].

---

[122]https://bitcoinmagazine.com/articles/ozcoin-hacked-stolen-funds-seized-and-returned-by-strongcoin-1366822516/

Risks:

1. **Funds Loss**. Though it's certainly possible that an institutional thief at a bank doesn't know what he's getting, most likely he is a sophisticated thief who is looking for private keys in order to steal the funds.

Process Solutions:

1. **Monitor the Industry**. Read Bitcoin news sites or use a system like Google Alerts to receive relevant news, so that you can be aware of happenings in the Bitcoin industry, particularly security compromises.
2. **Monitor Your Funds**. Regularly monitor funds to make sure they're not disappearing. Make sure that alarms are obtrusive. Have a plan in place to quickly save remaining funds if some disappear.

Cold Storage Solutions:

1. **Create Tamper Evidence**. Store keys or other secret materials in tamper-evident bags; place padlocks on your Cryptosteel. *Dangers: Process Fatigue.*
2. **Obscure or Protect Your Keys**. Store keys in an obscured way that would be readily obvious to the asset holder, but not to a thief. Alternatively, protect keys with a PIN or other code. *Dangers: Key Fragility.*
3. **Cold Storage Scenario Optional Steps:** Use Bags (Tamper-Evident), Seal Metal Tiles, Use Metal Enhancement (Redundant Metal Devices).

Hot Wallet Solutions:

1. **Create Cold Storage Procedure**. Adapt a **Cold Storage Procedure** that moves some or all of your funds off of your hot wallet. Only keep keys on an exchange or brokerage for the minimum amount of time required to make a transaction. *Dangers: Disaster, Casual Physical Theft.*
2. **Question Policies & Procedures**. Know the security policies and procedures of any company that you're working with; be sure that they have rigorous, well-documented security procedures that they follow religiously, and that they treat any variance from their procedure as a problem that must be investigated. Also, be sure that there are no negative policies that might affect your usage of its services.

Adversary: Internal Theft

Motivation. "You trusted me with your private keys. I intend to violate that trust because I want to steal your funds for my own use. And, I'll do my best to cover it up."

Key Words: Active.

A person trusted with private keys could steal funds. This might be an asset holder's heir or executor; within a corporate setting, it could be one of the persons trusted to use the keys or someone using social hacking to convince or coerce a trusted person to do the wrong thing. This is a difficult situation because the asset holder has typically trusted someone with a key because they need to have it in order to do their job. The problem is that the trust was mislaid or coercion was used.

Historic Case Study: Stealing from Shapeshift. Shapeshift.io's IT lead stole 315 bitcoins from them, then fled. However, that wasn't the end of the story. Afterward, he sold information about the company's security to a hacker, initiating a second breach, then sold the hacker access to a backdoor he'd installed, creating a third. **News Story**[123].

Historic Case Study: Walking the Silk Road. While investigating Silk Road, Secret Service agent Shaun Bridges gained the login credentials of an admin and used them to steal 20,000 Bitcoins from Silk Road by transferring them to Mt. Gox. He then moved his funds from Mt. Gox just before the US government seized $2.1 million dollars worth of Mt. Gox funds. He then stole another 1,600 bitcoins that had been seized from Bitstamp — this time *after* being found guilty to the first crime! **News Story**[124], **News Story**[125], **News Story**[126].

---

[123]https://news.bitcoin.com/looting-fox-sabotage-shapeshift/
[124]https://arstechnica.com/tech-policy/2015/12/rogue-secret-service-agent-who-stole-from-silk-road-sentenced-to-nearly-6-years/
[125]https://motherboard.vice.com/en_us/article/vv7dgj/great-moments-in-shaun-bridges-a-corrupt-silk-road-investigator
[126]https://arstechnica.com/tech-policy/2017/11/ex-agent-corrupted-by-silk-road-sentenced-to-2-additional-years/

Risks

1. **Funds Loss**. Since the untrustworthy person knows exactly what they're getting and how to use it, the end result is obviously the theft of your funds.

Process Solutions:

1. **Create Paper Trails**. Leave records for all access to funds. Make this a required part of a procedure.
2. **Limit Funds Spending**. Use smart custody options to limit what funds can be spent at one time. *Dangers: User Error.*
3. **Monitor Your Funds**. Regularly monitor funds to make sure they're not disappearing. Make sure that alarms are obtrusive. Have a plan in place to quickly save remaining funds if some disappear.
4. **Use Funds Multisignatures**. Lock funds with a multisignature, which requires two or more people (possibly from a larger group of people) to sign off for use of funds. *Dangers: Internal Theft, User Error .*
5. **Use Funds Timelocks**. Lock funds with a timelock, which doesn't allow a specific person to access the funds until a specific time. Create a regular procedure to update the timelock as it nears expiration. *Dangers: User Error.*

Cold Storage Solutions:

1. **Cold Storage Scenario Optional Steps**: Seal Metal Tiles, Use Bags (Tamper-Evident), Use Metal Enhancement (Redundant Metal Devices).

Adversary: Network Attack, Personal

Motivation. *"I know you personally have cryptocurrency, and I want to steal it. I will use my expertise with programming or with hacking to attack you on the internet, and then your bitcoin will be mine."*

Alternative Categories: Computer Error.

Key Words: Active, Hot Wallet, Technological.

A networked attack against an specific person or company's cryptocurrency holdings. A hacker may eavesdrop or change data on a site or *en route* to a site. For Bitcoin transactions, they might try to change the recipient of a transaction or they might try to access the credentials of the asset holder, so that they can generate a transaction as they see fit. They could also try to hack into the site where the private keys are held.

Abstract Case Study: Eavesdropping on Wifi. Alice connects to the free wi-fi network at the airport. When she goes to her Javascript web wallet, she gets a certificate warning and ignores it, because those things pop up all the time. She doesn't realize that Eve is intercepting all connections to this wallet at the airport and has just compromised her wallet's credentials. Bob uses the same free wi-fi at the airport and connects to the same web wallet. Except, Bob never types in the "https://" at the front of his URL; he expects his browser to fill it in for him. As a result he *doesn't* get any warning when Eve intercepts his connection on the unchanged "http://" URL.

Historic Case Study: Spoofing Bitcointalk. An attacker forged a fax to a domain registrar to take control of the Bitcointalk domain. After doing so they pointed it to CloudFlare and were able to get a new SSL cert issued for the domain. Connections to Bitcointalk now went to the CloudFlare proxy, which stole any credentials before going back to Bitcointalk. The attacker didn't care about the Bitcointalk credentials, but assumed the same logins and passwords would be used at other sites such as Bitcoin exchanges. They were foiled by the fact that the proxy immediately collapsed under the Bitcointalk load and the Bitcointalk admins then noticed and figured out the problem.

Historic Case Study: Hacking Coinbase Accounts. A CEO of an internet startup decided to move some of his investments to cryptocurrency. For his digital currency exchange, he chose Coinbase, a site that had never been hacked. His Coinbase account was linked to his Gmail account, itself protected with 2FA linked to his cell phone. Despite all of those protections, hackers attacked the CEO by going after the weakest link in the chain: his T-Mobile cellphone account. They moved his cell phone number to a different device, used that to retrieve Google's two-factor authentication messages, and used that to break into Coinbase. He isn't the only user who's been actively targeted in this way. **News Story**[127].

---

[127]http://fortune.com/2017/08/22/bitcoin-coinbase-hack/

Risks:

1. **Funds Loss.** The ultimate goal of an Personal Network Attack is usually funds theft, but that can occur via several means.

a) **Account Compromise.** In a masquerade attack, an Personal Network Attacker might take control of your account at a Bitcoin brokerage or exchange, giving them access to any keys and any records or logs stored there.
b) **Transaction Corruption.** In an en-route attack, an Personal Network Attacker might corrupt a transaction that you have in process, misdirecting it.
2. **Cascade: Correlation.** If an attacker gains access to logs or records, they can probably trace an asset holder's usage of funds.
3. **Cascade: Transaction Error.** If an attacker manages to substitute a recipient address, the user will send funds to the wrong place.

Process Solutions:

1. **Maintain Emergency Procedure.** Write a procedure that describes what to do if your security has been compromised. Follow it quickly and precisely. Generally, move funds if their keys have any possibility of compromise. *Dangers: Process Fatigue.*
2. **Monitor Your Funds.** Regularly monitor funds to make sure they're not disappearing. Make sure that alarms are obtrusive. Have a plan in place to quickly save remaining funds if some disappear.
3. **Practice Anonymity.** Do not let people know you have bitcoins; ensure that you in no way ever link your key to your real persona.

Hot Wallet Solutions:

1. **Create Cold Storage Procedure.** Adapt a **Cold Storage Procedure** that moves some or all of your funds off of your hot wallet. Only keep keys on an exchange or brokerage for the minimum amount of time required to make a transaction. *Dangers: Disaster, Casual Physical Theft.*
2. **Maintain Account Security.** Be sure that all online accounts have very robust passwords and that the companies have high security ratings.
3. **Practice Session Security.** Ensure that all online communications are encrypted.

Cold Storage Solutions:

1. **Cold Storage Scenario Optional Steps:** Use a USB Drive.

Adversary: Network Attack, Systemic

Motivation. *"I'm a big kahuna among hackers. I don't go after your little bitcoin wallets, I go after the exchanges or other bitcoin sites instead. Nonetheless, you might just find yourself at a literal loss when I bankrupt the company holding your wallet."*

Alternative Categories: Computer Error.

Key Words: Active, Hot Wallet, Technological.

Users are usually most concerned about Personal Network Attacks which target them directly; due to the decentralized nature of Bitcoin, each user is their own last line of defense. However, hackers might instead decide to go after the companies that users are working with. This is both a big danger, because it's been a prime source for Bitcoin intrusions, and a big problem, because the user doesn't have any control over this level of infrastructure.

Historic Case Study: Unsigning the Transactions. In the early days of Bitcoin, there were sites that processed transactions, but which had bugs in their code. It was possible to send some of them invalid, unsigned transactions, and they would still think they had gotten paid. Some of these early sites were taken advantage of, and their customers lost money.

Historic Case Study: Bankrupting Betcoin Dice. Hackers took over Ghash.io, giving them about 25-30% of network hashing power. They mined a block that gave Ghash's funds to themselves, but before they announced it, they made a bunch of bets at Betcoin Dice. Some paid out, then Ghash announced a block that reversed the bets, effectively creating a double spend. Betcoin Dice lost 1000 bitcoins. **Forum Post**[128].

Historic Case Study: Filling the Graveyard. Many other blockchains has suffered systemic network attacks over the years. **Blockchain Graveyard**[129]. One recent report states that there were more than $900 million dollars in losses, most of them from Systemic Attacks, just in the first nine months of 2018. **CoinDesk**[130].

---

[128]https://bitcointalk.org/index.php?topic=327767.0
[129]https://magoo.github.io/Blockchain-Graveyard/
[130]https://www.coindesk.com/nearly-1-billion-stolen-in-crypto-hacks-so-far-this-year-research

Risks:

1. **Funds Loss.** Though it's a company being attacked, if they lose their cash, and can't recover it through insurance claims, this directly impacts the users.

2. **Key Denial or Key Loss.** Attackers might deny users temporary or permanent access to their online keys, even if they're not able to access those keys themselves.

3. **Cascade: Correlation.** Attackers who have taken over a site can do all kinds of nefarious things, such as spy upon users and correlate their various addresses.

Process Solutions:

1. **Maintain Emergency Procedure.** Write a procedure that describes what to do if your security has been compromised. Follow it quickly and precisely. Generally, move funds if their keys have any possibility of compromise. *Dangers: Process Fatigue.*

2. **Monitor the Industry.** Read Bitcoin news sites or use a system like Google Alerts to receive relevant news, so that you can be aware of happenings in the Bitcoin industry, particularly security compromises.

Hot Wallet Solutions:

1. **Create Cold Storage Procedure.** Adapt a **Cold Storage Procedure** that moves some or all of your funds off of your hot wallet. Only keep keys on an exchange or brokerage for the minimum amount of time required to make a transaction. *Dangers: Disaster, Casual Physical Theft.*

2. **Maintain Account Security.** Be sure that all online accounts have very robust passwords and that the companies have high security ratings.

3. **Question Policies & Procedures.** Know the security policies and procedures of any company that you're working with; be sure that they have rigorous, well-documented security procedures that they follow religiously, and that they treat any variance from their procedure as a problem that must be investigated. Also, be sure that there are no negative policies that might affect your usage of its services.

Cold Storage Solutions:

1. **Cold Storage Scenario Optional Steps:** Use a (Second) USB Drive.

Adversary: Physical Theft, Casual

Motivation. "*I just want an easy score, and your house looks like it. Obviously, I'm taking your jewelry and your electronics. But, if you got a safe, I'll try to take that too. I have no idea what I'll do with it, or with the contents if I can get it open. If I see some weird numbers, I'll probably just trash them.*"

Key Words: Active, Cold Storage, Physical.

An entirely opportunistic real-world theft could, by chance, scoop up private keys. This is typically a burglary or a robbery that results in the acquisition of a computer device or safe that happens to contain private keys, but which weren't the motivation for the theft. Casual Theft often results in denial rather than loss.

Abstract Case Study: Waiting for the Other Shoe. Dan's house is broken into. His electronics are stolen, including his laptop. Though his bitcoin keys are on the laptop, and his procedure says he should now move his funds as soon as possible, he doesn't worry about it because the whole hard drive is encrypted. A few months later, his bitcoins all disappear in the night.

Abstract Case Study: Losing a Phone. Bob accidently leaves his phone in his car, and a thief breaks the window and steals it. The phone contains Bob's old Bitcoin wallet; it used to only have "play" money, but due to the increase in the value of Bitcoin it is now worth $50 thousand dollars. Bob can't remember where he kept his recovery phrase.

Risks:

1. **Key Loss**. Because the physical representation of the key has been taken, it will no longer be available to the asset holder.

2. **Cascade: Sophisticated Theft**. A casual theft could lead to Sophisticated Theft if the thief realizes what he has and how to use it.

Process Solutions:

1. **Maintain Emergency Procedure**. Write a procedure that describes what to do if your security has been compromised. Follow it quickly and precisely. Generally, move funds if their keys have any possibility of compromise. *Dangers: Process Fatigue.*

Cold Storage Solutions:

1. **Obscure or Protect Your Keys**. Store keys in an obscured way that would be readily obvious to the asset holder, but not to a thief. Alternatively, protect keys with a PIN or other code. *Dangers: Key Fragility.*

2. **Redundantly Store Your Keys**. Maintain multiple representations of your master keys. Store encrypted keys in local storage and unencrypted keys in more protected storage, such as a safety deposit box. *Dangers: Casual Physical Theft, Institutional Theft.*

Adversary: Physical Theft, Sophisticated

Motivation. *"I know you have cryptocurrency and I want to steal your keys. I'm not a fancy hacker, email spoofer, or spear phisher. Instead, I'm someone who can successfully stage a real-world crime. I'll break into your house or your safety deposit box. Cut the music for my heist scene."*

Key Words: Active, Cold Storage, Physical.

Unlike a Casual Theft, a Sophisticated Theft is a real-world crime that specifically targets cryptocurrency keys. They could be going after computers, hardware wallets, CryptoTags, or some other storage that contains a key.

Abstract Case Study: Listening In. Mallory rents a suite next to a Bitcoin bank. He then sets up listening devices to engage in an EMI side channel attack, extracting crucial information from electromagnetic leaks.

Abstract Case Study: An Evil Maid Attacking. Bob leaves his computer in his hotel room, and Mallory, now masquerading as a maid, sneaks in and installs a keylogger, possibly after booting from a corrupted USB stick. When Bob .ater types in his encryption keys, they'll be sucked up by the keylogger and available to Mallory.

Risks:

1. **Funds Loss.** The goal of the thief is to acquire private keys so that he can then steal the funds associated with them.
2. **Key Loss.** Technically a thief might physically steal private keys. However, that's really the least of the problems with a sophisticated theft. Because the private keys were purposefully stolen, the goal of the attacker is to acquire the related funds as soon as possible. Thus, the fact that the asset holder no longer has access to a key becomes quickly irrelevant.

Process Solutions:

1. **Maintain Emergency Procedure.** Write a procedure that describes what to do if your security has been compromised. Follow it quickly and precisely. Generally, move funds if their keys have any possibility of compromise. *Dangers: Process Fatigue.*
2. **Practice Anonymity.** Do not let people know you have bitcoins; ensure that you in no way ever link your key to your real persona.
3. **Use Paranoid Key Procedures.** Take extreme protective methods when generating keys or when accessing accounts. Turn off phones. Remove cell phones. Unplug electronics. Cover windows. Tape your computer's camera and muffle your microphone. Do not work in rooms adjacent to property that you don't own. In extreme cases, rent a random car in a far remote location to serve both as a faraday cage and as protection against observation. *Dangers: Process Fatigue.*

Cold Storage Solutions:

1. **Create Tamper Evidence.** Store keys or other secret materials in tamper-evident bags; place padlocks on your Cryptosteel. *Dangers: Process Fatigue.*
2. **Obscure or Protect Your Keys.** Store keys in an obscured way that would be readily obvious to the asset holder, but not to a thief. Alternatively, protect keys with a PIN or other code. *Dangers: Key Fragility.*
3. **Cold Storage Scenario Optional Steps:** Use Bags (Tamper-Evident).

Adversary: Social Engineering

Motivation. *"I'm the thief who doesn't get my hands dirty. Instead, I'm a confidence man who tricks you into doing my dirty work for me. Maybe I talk with you in person or on the phone, or maybe I steal in bulk by spamming out phishing messages. In either case, my goal is to get access to your credentials or your computer and go from there."*

Key Words: Active.

The in-person confidence man is largely gone, but everyone in the modern world is constantly barraged by fake tech-support calls and phishing emails that attempt to trick us into either revealing our logins and passwords or else installing malware on our machines. From there, the social engineers can roll out keyloggers, jump into accounts, and drain cryptocurrency funds.

Historic Case Study: Spearphishing Bitpay. An attacker *spearphished*[131] Bitpay, contacting the CFO and pretending to be an associate in the Bitcoin industry in order to convince them to login to a phishing page where the CFO revealed his Bitpay credentials. These credentials were then used to contact the CEO of Bitpay and convince him to transfer 5,000 Bitcoins, then worth $1.8 million dollars, over the course of three emails. **News Story**[132].

Abstract Case Study: Staging a BitCON. Mallory befriends Carol and convinces her to demonstrate how Bitcoin works. Mallory is able to spy out enough specifics about Carol's Bitcoin accounts that she's later able to break into them.

Historic Case Study: Poisoning Ads. The COINHOARDER group focused its phishing on poisoned advertisements, which linked to fake exchange sites using lookalike names such as blockchien.info and block-clain.info. This allowed them to steal credentials for use on the real site. **Analysis**[133].

---

[131]https://en.wikipedia.org/wiki/Phishing#Spear_phishing
[132]https://cointelegraph.com/news/bitpay-hacked-for-over-18-million-in-bitcoins
[133]https://blog.talosintelligence.com/2018/02/coinhoarder.html

Risks:

1. **Funds Loss**. The end-game of any social engineering attack focused on cryptocurrency is going to be the theft of your funds, and it's most likely to happen very quickly.

Process Solutions:

1. **Maintain Emergency Procedure**. Write a procedure that describes what to do if your security has been compromised. Follow it quickly and precisely. Generally, move funds if their keys have any possibility of compromise. *Dangers: Process Fatigue.*

2. **Practice Anonymity**. Do not let people know you have bitcoins; ensure that you in no way ever link your key to your real persona.

3. **Proactively Visit Sites**. Never reactively visit sites in response to instructions from a phone call, email, or other communication. Instead, always type a site name by hand. If necessary, get yourself out of an acute situation, such as speaking with someone on the phone, before you access a site.

4. **Take the Time**. Be very careful when you're working. Double-check everything. Don't take transferring large amounts of funds lightly, ever.

5. **Use Funds Multisignatures**. Lock funds with a multisignature, which requires two or more people (possibly from a larger group of people) to sign off for use of funds. *Dangers: Internal Theft, User Error.*

Adversary: Supply-Chain Attack

Motivation. *"I'm the slyest of thieves because I worm my way into your life without your even knowing. I corrupt your hardware before it gets to you. My goal is to mess with your devices so that I can mess with your digital assets, and you may never figure out how I did it!"*

Key Words: Active, Physical, Technological.

A supply-chain attack depends on corrupting a hardware wallet, computer, or other piece of hardware that's used in the digital-asset ecosystem *before* it ever gets to its user. Most likely, this is the job of a fraudulent middleman such as a hardware-wallet reseller, but it could be anyone in the supply chain from the original manufacturer to the postal delivery service. Obviously, you have to trust *someone*, which means that overcoming a supply-chain attack requires figuring out *who* to trust.

Historic Case Study: wallet.failing? Multiple security experts have pointed out the dangers of an attacker accessing a hardware wallet before it reaches the hands of a user. One expert inserted an RF chip to remotely trigger transactions while another noted that non-random seeds could be generated by a compromised hardware wallet. **News**[134], **Analysis**[135].

Historic Case Study: Distrusting Computers. When a certain individual was attempting to prove that he was Satoshi Nakamoto, Gavin Andresen was well aware of possible supply-chain attacks, so he required that tests be done on a "completely new, clean" computer. As required, the computer was delivered to Andresen in a "factory-sealed" box, but it was delivered by an administrative assistant employed by the other individual, which means that the supply chain could still have been compromised. **News**[136].

---

[134]https://threatpost.com/cryptocurrency-wallet-hacks-spark-dustup/140445/

[135]https://saleemrashid.com/2018/03/20/breaking-ledger-security-model/

[136]https://www.forbes.com/sites/ktorpey/2018/02/27/man-who-claimed-to-be-bitcoins-creator-may-be-asked-to-prove-it-in-10-billion-lawsuit/#1c4abef733d6

Risks:

1. **Funds Loss.** If someone is going to the trouble of corrupting your supply chain, they're probably doing it so that they can steal your money.
2. **Key Loss.** However, they potentially have complete control over your hardware, so maybe they'll just destroy your keys.

Process Solutions:

1. **Buy from Manufacturers.** Purchase hardware that will be used to protect digital assets directly from the manufacturers, to minimize the chance of middle-men corrupting the hardware.
2. **Minimize the Supply Chain.** Ensure that there are as few steps as possible in the purchase and delivery of any hardware used to protect your digital assets. If you could personally acquire hardware directly from the manufacturing floor, that would be ideal; practically, reduce in-between steps as much as you can.
3. **Practice Anonymity.** Do not let people know you have bitcoins; ensure that you in no way ever link your key to your real persona.

Cold Storage Solutions:

1. **Use Well-Known Hardware.** Ensure that any hardware used for your cold storage is manufactured by a well-known, well-trusted, and top-tier manufacturer.
2. **Cold Storage Scenario Optional Steps:** Erase Your Ledger(s), Use a USB Drive.

Category: Loss by Crime, Other Attacks

Origin. *Criminals.*

Definition. *A loss caused by some criminal act other than explicit theft.* Some crimes go larger scale, threatening you and yours, rather than just taking your money without your involvement. Alternatively, some crimes go in different directions, criminally depriving you of your cryptocurrency without the criminals taking it for themselves.

Iconic Image. *A man in a long overcoat with a gun.* Just as most people fear theft over other types of cryptocurrency loss, they really fear violence leading to theft, which is the main sort of escalated crime that is found in this listing of other criminal attacks.

Ulterior Motive. *Mixed.* For escalated theft, the ulterior motive is greed, but other sorts of crime can have more complex causes, from mischievousness to hacktivism to malice.

Adversary: Blackmail

Motivation. *"I'm holding something hostage. Perhaps I know something about you that you want to remain private. Perhaps I've encrypted your data or stolen your information. The point is, I'm going to do something very bad with what I'm holding unless you give me what I want. And what I want is money! Delivered to an anonymous account, of course."*

Key Words: Active.

Blackmail is ultimately a second-tier crime. The criminal has already gotten something you want, whether it be something he stole or just his silence. Now, he wants to convert that item into money. He's chosen cryptocurrency as his payment method because it's harder to trace it to a real person. Maybe he knows you have cryptocurrency, and that makes you a particularly juicy target. Or maybe he doesn't care. To date, the most well-known internet Blackmail schemes have tended to be assembly-line productions, involving phishing emails or worms sent to lots of users: like spam, they've succeeded based solely on volume.

The difference between Blackmail and Coercion is that Blackmail tends to be less physically threatening.

Historical Case Study: Encrypting Your Drive. Ransomware has been a prime attack vector for malware in recent years. The malware encrypts a hard drive, and the victim is told that they'll only get their data back if they pay a ransom in Bitcoins. **Analysis**[137].

Historical Case Study: Rooting Your Camera. Some blackmail is based on pure bluffing, such as the "sextortion" scam that has been circling the internet for a few years. Spam emails claim to have rooted the victim's camera, and threaten to release embarrassing pictures of a sexual nature taken with the camera. They have no basis in fact, but newer versions try and lend credence to the claim by including one of the victim's passwords in the email, a password that was collected via some other means. Allegedly, the only way to avoid the release of the pictures is payment of Bitcoins. **Analysis**[138].

---

[137]https://nakedsecurity.sophos.com/2019/02/14/inside-a-gandcrab-targeted-ransomware-attack-on-a-hospital/
[138]https://www.eff.org/deeplinks/2018/07/sextortion-scam-what-do-if-you-get-latest-phishing-spam-demanding-bitcoin

Risks:

1. **Continued Blackmail.** The biggest risk of blackmail is more blackmail. If an attacker feels that you're vulnerable, they'll do their best to exploit that vulnerability, again and again. Giving in to blackmail is rarely the right answer.
2. **Information Loss.** Of course, if you don't give in to blackmail, you might lose information that's been stolen or encrypted.
3. **Reputation Loss.** Alternatively, you might encourage the release of information that's embarrassing.
4. **Funds Loss.** On the flip side, if you give in to the blackmail, you're losing funds.

Process Solutions:

1. **Practice Anonymity.** Do not let people know you have bitcoins; ensure that you in no way ever link your key to your real persona.
2. **Protect Your Information.** Ensure that your critical information has strong protection, particularly backups; and if there is some embarrassing information out there, do what you can to either quash it or embrace it.

See Related Adversaries — Coercion

Adversary: Coercion

Motivation. *"I know you have cryptocurrency. Well, I've got power in the real world. I can threaten you, your family, your friends, your home, or your business — and, I can follow through on those threats! I want to get what you have, and I'm going to force you to give it to me by any means necessary."*

Key Words: Active, Physical.

An entity, whether it be a nation-state, a terrorist group, the mob, or a smart mugger, can threaten a cryptocurrency holder with the goal of forcing them to give away their funds (or in some other way corrupt the cryptocurrency market). Though there are solutions that absolutely prevent this sort of coercion from succeeding, they also place the victim in danger of the risks being carried out anyway, especially if the activated solutions are not understood by the public beforehand and are not provably activated. Often the best solution is to cooperate, or at least to seem to cooperate, in order to avoid severe consequences.

The difference between Blackmail and Coercion is that Coercion tends to be less focused on properties, reputations, and other non-physical elements.

Abstract Case Study: SWATing. Over the course of a month, Dan's power and his DSL line are turned off. He contacts the utilities and is told that these occurred at his request. He then receives an email that says, "we know where you live, send us half your bitcoins or next time we swat you and maybe you end up dead." A picture of his house from Google Street View is included.

Historical Case Study: Kidnapping. Ukranian cryptocurrency exchange executive Pavel Lerner was grabbed off the street outside his office, and held in an undisclosed location. He was told that he would not be released unless he paid $1 million dollars in bitcoins. **News Story**[139]. A similar kidnapping occurred in Dubai and resulted in the transfer of 25 BTC. **News Story**[140]. **Other Physical Attacks**[141].

---

[139]https://cointelegraph.com/news/kidnapping-of-bitcoin-exchange-executive-showed-importance-of-financial-privacy
[140]https://www.khaleejtimes.com/news/crime-and-courts/3-fake-dubai-cops-kidnap-traders-/to-rob-bitcoins
[141]https://github.com/jlopp/physical-bitcoin-attacks

Risks:

1. **Death.** An asset holder's life could be threatened if they do not comply.
2. **Funds Loss.** The goal of coercion is usually to steal funds.
3. **Physical Damage.** An asset holder could be threatened with torture or permanent disability if they do not comply.
4. **Physical Detention.** An asset holder could be kidnapped and held until they comply.

Process Solutions:

1. **Create False Funds.** Create a lesser cache of funds to be given over in case of coercion. Some hardware wallets support this with a "plausible deniability" or "alternate passphrase" function.
2. **Limit Funds Spending.** Use smart custody options to limit what funds can be spent at one time. *Dangers: User Error.*
3. **Practice Anonymity.** Do not let people know you have bitcoins; ensure that you in no way ever link your key to your real persona.
4. **Use Funds Multisignatures.** Lock funds with a multisignature, which requires two or more people (possibly from a larger group of people) to sign off for use of funds. *Dangers: Internal Theft, User Error.*
5. **Use Funds Timelocks.** Lock funds with a timelock, which doesn't allow a specific person to access the funds until a specific time. Create a regular procedure to update the timelock as it nears expiration. *Dangers: User Error.*
6. **Require Public Interaction.** Cross thresholds that put an adversary at risk. Store one of the necessary keys at a physical location where interactions with other people can be judged for signs of coercion. Include the presence or status of your loved ones in the judgements. Establish code words that actually mean, "Help"! Make the procedure slow enough that help could arrive. *Dangers: Process Fatigue.*

See Related Adversaries — Blackmail, Nation-State Actor, Terrorist / Mob

Adversary: Non-Financially Motivated Attackers

Motivation. *"I don't care about your money, but I'll still going to mess with you. Maybe I'm your enemy, who wants revenge or to out you in some way. Maybe you just have something I want — be it an artifact, a job, or some knowledge. The key is: I know who you are, I know what you have, and I want to use that knowledge as a lever for my own purposes."*

Key Words: *Active.*

Attackers may not care about acquiring your cryptocurrency, but could instead have other motives, such as wanting to reveal your transactions or wanting to keep you from accessing your own funds. Or, they could have totally alien motives: never imagine that you understand why a non-financially motivated attacker does the things he does!

Nature is the ultimate non-financially motivated attacker. It introduces pure chaos. Given enough time, it might do anything that a financially motivated attacker could!

Abstract Case Study: Infecting the Machines. Trudy writes malware that infects and crashes peoples' computers. No reason. She just enjoys knowing that she's ruining the lives of people who are too stupid to defend themselves. Dan has his bitcoins on a computer that is hit by Trudy's newest virus.

Historic Case Study: Destroying Parity. Parity multisigs wallets for Ethereum all depended upon a single code library; because of flaws in the code, a regular user was able to take ownership of the library, then destroy it. This caused $280 million dollars in Ethereum funds to be locked up. The actual motive of the attacker isn't known. He claims it was a beginner mistake, but it also could have been a malicious attack or a poorly considered attempt to steal funds. **News Story**[142], **Twitter Feed**[143].

---

[142]https://medium.com/chain-cloud-company-blog/parity-multisig-hack-again-b46771eaa838
[143]https://twitter.com/devops199?lang=en

Risks:

1. **Cascade: Correlation**. Some non-financially motivated attackers may be trying to determine who you are and what you're doing with your cryptocurrency.
2. **Cascade: Censorship**. Some non-financially motivated attackers may just want to keep you from accessing your funds.
3. **Cascade: Key Loss**. Some non-financially motivated attackers may just be destructive.

Process Solutions:

1. **Practice Anonymity.** Do not let people know you have bitcoins; ensure that you in no way ever link your key to your real persona.

Adversary: Terrorist / Mob

Motivation. *"I want your money and I am willing to kill, maim, or destroy to get it. Plus, I've got a reputation to uphold. If you force me to, I will have to do bad stuff. I ain't worried about the legal repercussions, because I'm already subverting the whole system."*

Key Words: *Active, Physical.*

In large part, a terrorist or mob adversary is a special case of the "coercion" adversary. A terrorist organization or an organized crime organization is likely to use coercion to acquire cryptocurrency funds, but they're more likely than most to carry through on mortal threats if they are foiled via various Smart Custody solutions that can be used to protect cryptocurrency from coercive threats. On the flip-side, since they're innately criminal organizations, a nation-state might offer protection against them.

Abstract Case Study: Killing Uncle Bob. Alice is too open about her bitcoin holdings, and the local mob finds out. Mallory, a representative of the mob, tells her that they'll kill her Uncle Bob if she doesn't make a payment of 10 bitcoins to a specific address. She refuses and they kill Uncle Bob.

Risks:

1. **Cascade: Blackmail.** The threats of a criminal adversary could be blackmail.
2. **Cascade: Coercion.** Or they could be coercive in a more damaging way.

Process Solutions:

1. **Practice Anonymity.** Do not let people know you have bitcoins; ensure that you in no way ever link your key to your real persona.
2. **Register Your Funds.** Register and document your funds fully with your nation-state to maximize legal protections. *Dangers: Legal Forfeiture, Nation-State Actor.*

See Related Adversaries — Blackmail, Coercion

Category: Loss by Government

Origin. *Government.*

Definition. *A loss caused by the government exerting its sovereign rights.* The government can just take your money if they want, perhaps by arbitrary edict, perhaps through espionage, perhaps as part of a legal process.

Iconic Image. *A man in black, wearing sunglasses.* Many people turn to cryptocurrency due to a loss of faith in the government, symbolized by the iconic men in black, who spies on the government's citizens. However, it's much more likely that you could lose your money in a court case, when the judge hands down a verdict.

Ulterior Motive. *Authority.* If you lose your cryptocurrency to the government, it's ultimately a sign of their executive, judicial, or legislative authority. They take your cryptocurrency because they can — and perhaps because they must, to maintain that authority.

Adversary: Legal Forfeiture

Motivation. *"I desire your funds, please, but only because I am rightfully owed them. You violated a contract, neglected to pay a bill, or were held liable for a tort. So, pay up."*

Key Words: *Active.*

Just like any other asset, cryptocurrency can be subject to legal forfeiture. This is usually not considered an issue, under the assumption that forfeiture as part of a civic lawsuit or state action is legal. However, it becomes very problematic if a nation-state is corrupt and has been bribed by a party to a lawsuit or is attacking the asset holder illegally, for its own self-interest. Even a legitimate nation-state might allow its citizens to fall prey to fraudulent lawsuits.

Abstract Case Study: Extorting Legally.
Mallory discovers that Carol has bitcoins. She walks up to her door on an cold day where there's ice on the ground and *whoops* falls down. She soon has a doctor proclaiming that she's been crippled for life. Mallory then uses the legal system to seize Carol's bitcoins.

Risks:

1. **Funds Loss.** Obviously the danger of legal forfeiture is the loss of the funds themselves.
2. **Cascade: Denial of Access.** A legal forfeiture can sometimes cause a purposeful denial of access to a house, safe, or safety deposit box.

Process Solutions:

1. **Neutrally Store Your Funds.** Maintain funds or keys outside of the sphere of control of fascist and authoritarian nation-states.
2. **Practice Anonymity.** Do not let people know you have bitcoins; ensure that you in no way ever link your key to your real persona.

Adversary: Nation-State Actor

Motivation. "I am the all-powerful state. I can do whatever I want to my citizens. I can surveil, I can seize. I can imprison, I can threaten. I can make their lives so awful that cryptocurrency is the least of their concerns. However, I am hopefully bound by laws and morality: if my citizens obey the rules and don't interact with criminals, and if I am truly a law-abiding nation, then they have nothing to worry about. I just want to keep my nation and its people safe."

Key Words: Active.

A nation-state could exert its tremendous power to corrupt the cryptocurrency market. This could be a surveillance threat, where a government is listening in on transactions, or it could be a coercive threat, where the state uses its authority to force a cryptocurrency holder into some action. Overall a nation-state has such expansive powers that almost all risks are possible, requiring almost all solutions.

More problematically, individuals might take on the mantle of the nation-state and use its powers in ways that are either abusive or illegal.

Abstract Case Study: Targeting Lawfully. Alice operates a Bitcoin business in China, where the currency has come under increasing scrutiny in recent years. She is not a financial institution, so she should be able to legally operate, but the grey area surrounding the currency in China leaves her vulnerable. Grace, a government operative, takes advantage of this. She needs information on one of Alice's customers and uses the questionable status of Bitcoin in the country to threaten Alice.

Historic Case Study: Stealing Safe Deposit Boxes. During a series of fiscal crises, the state of California reduced their time period for property to be considered abandoned to a paltry three years, and safety deposit boxes were then confiscated and auctioned off. Sufficiently aggressive banks began seizing safety deposit boxes that were unchecked, even when they remained in contact with the customer on other topics! Bitcoin keys stored in safety deposit boxes could be vulnerable to this malfeasance. **News Story**[144].

Risks:

1. **Key Loss.** A nation-state could purposefully seize private keys or they could casually do so while seizing electronics or safety deposit boxes.

---

[144]https://www.sfgate.com/cgi-bin/article.cgi?f=/c/a/2007/07/02/LOSTPROPERTY.TMP

2. **Cascade: Coercion**. Authoritarian action could lead to personal threat.

3. **Cascade: Correlation**. Surveillance could lead to the gathering of personally identifying information.

4. **Cascade: Legal Forfeiture**. Many of the concerns about a nation-state actor involve it working in illegal ways, but it could also choose to act within the constraints of its own legal system, sometimes by using surprise changes or favorable interpretations of vague laws.

Process Solutions:

1. **Neutrally Store Your Funds**. Maintain funds or keys outside of the sphere of control of fascist and authoritarian nation-states.

2. **Practice Anonymity**. Do not let people know you have bitcoins; ensure that you in no way ever link your key to your real persona.

3. **Use Paranoid Key Procedures**. Take extreme protective methods when generating keys or when accessing accounts. Turn off phones. Remove cell phones. Unplug electronics. Cover windows. Tape your computer's camera and muffle your microphone. Do not work in rooms adjacent to property that you don't own. In extreme cases, rent a random car in a far remote location to serve both as a faraday cage and as protection against observation. *Dangers: Process Fatigue*

Cold Storage Solutions:

1. **Obscure or Protect Your Keys**. Store keys in an obscured way that would be readily obvious to the asset holder, but not to a thief. Alternatively, protect keys with a PIN or other code. *Dangers: Key Fragility.*

2. **Widely Separate Your Keys**. Maintain multiple physical representations of your master keys in places that are widely separated. Consider locales under different legal jurisdictions and with different physical risks.

See Related Adversaries — Coercion

Category: Loss by Mistakes

Origin. YOU.

Definition. A loss caused by the user making an error. The most dangerous threat to your cryptocurrency is probably *you.* Most often this is the result of your making an easy but uncorrectable error, but it could also be due purposefully deciding not to follow the most secure procedures.

Iconic Image. A man with head on keyboard, weeping. The worst thing about a Loss by Mistake is that it's your fault: there's no one else to blame. And, there's often nothing that you can do about it afterward.

Ulterior Motive. None. Like an Act of God or Computer Error, there's no purposeful intent behind this loss of funds, just apathy, fatigue, distraction, or something else that keeps you from giving 100% to your cryptocurrency management. (Which is a good reason to only engage in your cryptocurrency management when you're in top form.)

Adversary: Convenience

Motivation. *"I know that you want things to be simple. I encourage that. Life should be easy. Don't use that tamper-evident bag. Don't keep your safety deposit box in another state, away from California's fault lines. And if you're going on a trip, definitely ease up on the security of your bitcoins, so that you can access them from the road. I'm sure nothing bad can happen from all of this ease of use!"*

Key Words: *Passive.*

Convenience can be the bane of any security procedure. It could be due to sheer laziness: because of Process Fatigue, a bitcoin holder might eliminate some of the more onerous elements of his procedure, such as the need to check his bitcoins twice a year, or the need to go out to a (potentially distant) safety deposit box to do so. However, there can also be real, pragmatic, and understandable reasons for increasing the Convenience of bitcoin access, despite the cost to security. A businessman going on a trip might ask for bitcoins to be moved from their normal multi-sig transaction to one that he can sign for alone, increasing his convenience of access, but opening up those bitcoins to any number of either adversaries.

Abstract Case Study: Trusting the Wrong Person. Alice is going to be out of town all month. She expects to make some very large bitcoin purchases during that time period, so she needs her coins more conveniently accessible than her normal cold storage procedure allows. She opts not to go with the convenience of carrying them on one of her electronic devices because she's afraid they could be seized. Instead, she gives her husband, Bob, access to her keys. When she calls up Bob to have him make a transaction, she finds his phone line disconnected. He's gone, with her bitcoin wealth!

Abstract Case Study: Trusting the Hot Wallet. After the divorce, Alice is a bit more savvy, and decides to move her money to a hot wallet while she's out of town. Unfortunately, hot wallets can be a lot more vulnerable than cold storage, so she loses her bitcoin wealth again!

Risks:

1. **Funds Loss**. The worst danger of increased Convenience is the loss of the coins that are no longer have strong protections.
2. **Key Loss**. Alternatively, less rigorous procedures could lead to the loss of keys.
3. **Cascade: Personal Network Attack**. Many convenience changes might take keys out of cold storage; this opens them up to Personal Network Attacks.
4. **Cascade: Coercion**. Increased access to coins could lead to increased vulnerability to coercion.
5. **Cascade: Theft, All**. Increased accessibility and decreased security might lead to more Casual, Institutional, Internal, or Sophisticated Thefts.
6. **Cascade: User Error**. Lower attention to details can make User Error more likely.

Process Solutions:

1. **Create Checklists**. Create simple checklists and print many copies. Physically check each box as you work down your list of procedures.
2. **Maximize Security**. Subject to the needs of Convenience and the dangers of Process Fatigue, maintain the best security possible for the situation.

See Related: Process Fatigue

Adversary: Key Fragility

Motivation. *"I am entropy writ small. All I need to do is mislay a digit or two from a ridiculously large number, and my job is done. Perhaps you could make my job easier by encoding or obscuring your key or by maintaining just a single copy; complexity and singularity both beget fragility in different ways.."*

Alternative Categories: *Computer Error.*

Key Words: *Cold Storage, Passive, Technological.*

A key may be lost because its complexity makes it innately prone to loss. This could be a physical loss, where the physical representation of the key is accidentally lost, misplaced, or destroyed. It could be a computer error, where a disk lost a file or a backup became unreliable. It could be a corruption at key generation; a scribing error, where the wrong key was written down; or a recovery corruption where the wrong key is recreated from an external source. When key storage is obscured or protected, it might not be the key itself that is lost, but instead the method to unobscure the key or the code to decode it.

Abstract Case Study: Losing Addresses. Alice generates an address on an exchange so that she can send funds there, and immediately sends bitcoins, but the exchange has a massive failure. The address is never recorded! Alice shows them that she sent the funds, but they have no record of the address, and she's unable to prove it's really theirs.

Historic Case Study: Breaking VanityGen. A patched version of the VanityGen address creator generated compressed keys. Unfortunately, there was a bug with how it padded out keys. 1 time in 256 when it serialized the private key, it would prepend a 0 to the address and lose the last byte.

Historic Case Study: Forgetting the PIN. A Wired author stored 7.4 BTC on a Trezor and protected it with a PIN. A cleaning service threw away the paper with the PIN, which also contained the recovery words. The author soon realized that he didn't remember the PIN and every time he entered it incorrectly, the Trezor doubled a timeout period before he could try again. **News Story**[145].

---

[145]https://www.wired.com/story/i-forgot-my-pin-an-epic-tale-of-losing-dollar30000-in-bitcoin/

Risks:

1. **Key Loss.** Whatever the exact means by which the key is lost or corrupted, it becomes unavailable.

Process Solutions:

1. **Redundantly Relay Your Secrets.** Tell someone else the secrets required to unobscure or unprotect your private keys or to access your funds. *Dangers: Internal Theft.*
2. **Take the Time.** Be very careful when you're working. Double-check everything. Don't take transferring large amounts of funds lightly, ever.
3. **Verify Your Keys.** Test that your key is correct by signing and verifying a test message using your key. If you're really paranoid, create a test transaction using your private key or create and send a small transaction from your funds. *Dangers: Correlation.*

Cold Storage Solutions:

1. **Redundantly Store Your Keys.** Maintain multiple representations of your master keys. Store encrypted keys in local storage and unencrypted keys in more protected storage, such as a safety deposit box. *Dangers: Casual Physical Theft, Institutional Theft.*
2. **Cold Storage Scenario Optional Steps:** Use Metal Enhancement (Redundant Metal Devices); Use a (USB) Laser Printer.

See Related Adversaries — Bitrot, Transaction Error, User Error

Adversary: Process Fatigue

Motivation. *"I am laziness and exhaustion. I want to encourage you to skip the most time-consuming steps of a procedure, because they're too much trouble. I want to introduce small errors as you go, because you're tired of this repetitive yet mindful task. I want to turn your procedure against itself, so that the very process intended to protect your funds causes you to lose them."*

Key Words: *Passive.*

A digital-asset process can be so complicated that it causes errors in the procedure or in the avoidance of it. This inattention can result in immediate problems such as incorrect recording of a private key, errors in moving funds, or inadvertent correlation. Alternatively, a complex procedure can be lost over time, as members who know the procedure leave and are replaced within an organization (a form of humancentric Bitrot!). These errors can also cascade into any number of other problems. Still, doing something is usually better than doing nothing.

Abstract Case Study: Losing a Key. Bob needs to go check his safety deposit box but discovers the safety deposit box key isn't where it belongs. Oh well! It'll surely turn up by next year.

Abstract Case Study: Refusing the Imperfect. Whenever she has some spare time, Carol works on her bitcoin storage procedure. She's trying to get it just right. Of course, while she's working on the procedure, her master seeds are being stored on a piece of paper jammed in a desk drawer.

Abstract Case Study: Waiting for the Right Time. A cryptocurrency company pays its employees a cryptocurrency bonus. Everyone gets cryptocurrency. However, some employees weren't ready to hold their bitcoins when they received their first bonus, so they asked the company to hold onto them. The company goes bankrupt.

Risks:

1. **Key Loss**. The most likely result of process fatigue is the loss of a key, which somehow becomes mislaid or corrupted due to the inattention to the procedure. This usually is the result of one of several possible cascades.
2. **Cascade: Bitrot**. Not regularly assessing and rotating key storage increases the chance of bitrot.
3. **Cascade: Key Fragility**. Not regularly testing keys also increases the chance of key fragility.
4. **Cascade: User Error**. Finally, the lack of attention to a procedure can increase the odds of user error.

Process Solutions:

1. **Check Your Work**. Double-check your work; even better, have someone else double-check your work; even better, have an official procedure requiring someone else to double-check your work.
2. **Create Checklists**. Create simple checklists and print many copies. Physically check each box as you work down your list of procedures.
3. **Minimize Your Process**. Choose a minimum number of adversaries, and use only the solutions related to those adversaries. Occasionally revisit your procedure and cut out any steps that are proving too difficult — but carefully consider the dangers that are reintroduced by doing so.

See Related: Convenience

Adversary: Transaction Error

Motivation. *"I am the slightest error in a transaction. I'm the script that can't complete, the address that goes to the wrong place, or even the fee that wasn't big enough. I want your transaction to do something that you don't expect. I am startling results that are ultimately detrimental to you."*

Alternative Categories: Computer Error.

Key Words: Passive, Technological.

Errors introduced into a transaction can lead to the loss of some or all funds. Though it is hard to simply mistype an address in Bitcoin, due to error-checking, there are other potential threats. A Transaction Error could be due to an Personal Network Attack (where an attacker substituted an address), or it could be due to system error (where a system produced an incorrect address).

There can be other transaction issues too, such as sending the wrong type of transaction (e.g., a P2PKH when a multisig or smart contract was intended) or paying too high of a fee or paying to a cryptocurrency fork.

The fundamental issue is lack of transparency in the address itself and in the overall transaction, both of which are natively represented as somewhat intimidating sets of letters and numbers. Anything that improves that transparency, or that tests those computer values, addresses this adversary.

Abstract Case Study: Copying the Wrong Address. Mallory spams the Bitcoin network with dust payments that lodge in users' wallets. Later, Frank moves some money. He intends to send it to one of his wallet own addresses, but when he's looking at his wallet, he accidentally copies Mallory's sender address rather than his own recipient address. The money transfer goes to Mallory.

Abstract Case Study: Waiting Out the Clock. Bob writes a script with a Timelock for a time of 1609459200, so that the transaction will unlock on January 1, 2021. Except he forgets the last digit, and instead sets it to 160945920. Since the lock time is less than 500 million it's interpreted as a blockheight; at a block every 10 minutes, those funds will become available again in a bit more than 3,000 years.

Abstract Case Study: Paying the Miners. Carol sends $100 (.01 BTC) from an old 1 BTC transaction that she got in the early days of the technology. She remembers to send the remainder to a change address, but is confused over the value of the original transaction and only sends herself .48 rather than the .98 BTC that she intended. She doesn't double-check her math, nor does she use an interface that does so. The happy miner of her transaction earns about $5,000 from her.

Historic Case Study: Hacking the CoinDash ICO. While CoinDash was conducting an ICO, hackers broke into their web site and replaced the funding address with one of their own. $7 million dollars in Ethereum were sent to the hackers instead of CoinDash. **News Story**[146].

Risks:

1. **Funds Delay.** The least problematic sorts of transaction error just lead to delayed funds, where you have to resend them when you realize that you messed up.

2. **Funds Loss.** In the worst cases, all of the funds could be lost due to sending it away or due to theft after not locking it with the intended sort of signature.

3. **Funds Vulnerability.** Locking a transaction with the wrong sort of signature can alternatively just make the funds more vulnerable: now, a single person can sign for them rather than multiple people.

4. **Partial Funds Loss.** A fee-related transaction error is an example of partial funds lost: Perhaps you paid $100 instead of $10 or $1 — though this is a situation where most interfaces have gotten better at preventing errors over time.

Process Solutions:

1. **Check Your Work.** Double-check your work; even better, have someone else double-check your work; even better, have an official procedure requiring someone else to double-check your work.

2. **Create Checklists.** Create simple checklists and print many copies. Physically check each box as you work down your list of procedures.

3. **Take the Time.** Be very careful when you're working. Double-check everything. Don't take transferring large amounts of funds lightly, ever.

4. **Verify Your Scripts.** Double-check that your script has valid responses. For large-scale funds held by a script, you may want to first test them with smaller amounts of funds. *Dangers: Correlation.*

5. **Verify Your Transactions.** Double-check the recipient addresses for any transactions. Make sure the change address really belongs to you. Make sure that the fee looks rational. Validate the transaction on testnet to verify it.

See Related Adversaries — Key Fragility, User Error .

---

[146]https://www.coindesk.com/7-million-ico-hack-results-coindash-refund-offer/

Adversary: User Error

Motivation. *"I'm that niggling mistake that wouldn't be a major problem in most financial situations. I want you to make a typo or to use the wrong address, so that you don't get your money or send it to the wrong place. I want you to lose your keys, so that you can't recover your funds. I am all the anxieties you have about Bitcoin made real."*

Key Words: *Passive.*

Funds could be lost due to a user mistake. This can overlap with Key Fragility if the asset holder doesn't correctly record his key; or with Transaction Error if the asset holder doesn't correctly record an address. However, there are other possible errors in the Bitcoin ecosystem such as falling for a phishing attempt or forgetting to pay for a safety deposit box. Many other adversaries can cascade from user errors, so be careful.

Abstract Case Study: Forgetting the PIN. Alice has heard of other people losing their PINs, but knows it can't happen to her. But then she types in the wrong PIN three times to her Ledger, and it erases her keys.

Abstract Case Study: Forgetting to Pay for a Safety Deposit Box: Dan has put his recovery phrase on a piece of paper that is located in his safe deposit box. He forgets to notify his bank of an address change, and they seize the contents of the box, shredding its paper contents as there are no valuables. *Unclaimed Property Article*[147].

---

[147]http://www.uppo.org/blogpost/925381/281568/Unclaimed-Safe-Deposit-Box-Basics

Risks:

1. **Funds Loss**. There's no arbiter on the Bitcoin network, so if an asset holder makes a mistake, funds can be irretrievably lost.

2. **Cascade: Key Fragility**. A User Error can cause incorrect key recording.

3. **Cascade: Transaction Error**. A User Error can cause incorrect address recording, or foul up other elements of a transaction.

Process Solutions:

1. **Check Your Work**. Double-check your work; even better, have someone else double-check your work; even better, have an official procedure requiring someone else to double-check your work.

2. **Create Checklists**. Create simple checklists and print many copies. Physically check each box as you work down your list of procedures.

3. **Take the Time**. Be very careful when you're working. Double-check everything. Don't take transferring large amounts of funds lightly, ever.

4. **Verify Your Keys**. Test that your key is correct by signing and verifying a test message using your key. If you're really paranoid, create a test transaction using your private key or create and send a small transaction from your funds. *Dangers: Correlation.*

5. **Verify Your Transactions**. Double-check the recipient addresses for any transactions. Make sure the change address really belongs to you. Make sure that the fee looks rational. Validate the transaction on testnet to verify it.

Cold Storage Scenario Optional Steps: None.

See Related Adversaries — Key Fragility, Transaction Error

Category: Privacy-related Problems

Origin. *Society.*

Definition. *A problem that costs you privacy, or a problem created by a lack of privacy.* Privacy problems come in two parts. First, you can lose privacy through various means (such as Correlation), and second that lack of privacy can cause you other problems (like Censorship or even the various Criminal acts discussed herein). The adversaries in this category encompass both of these possibilities.

Iconic Image. *A man hiding his nakedness with his hands.* Loss of privacy is innately embarrassing, but its problems can go far beyond that.

Ulterior Motive. *Mixed.* Someone might destroy privacy for any number of reasons, including curiosity, nosiness, or maliciousness. Once they've destroyed privacy, they might use that lack of anonymity for purposes of greed (e.g., blackmail), revenge, or pure sadism.

Adversary: Censorship

Motivation. *"I don't want your money, I just want to make sure you can't have it. But, I have a deeper motivation than that. Maybe I'm threatening you, maybe I'm blackmailing you, and maybe I'm getting my revenge. Whatever the case, I personally know you, I know you have cryptocurrency, and I'm making sure that you can't use it."*

Alternative Categories: Loss by Crime, Misc.

Key Words: Active, Technological.

An entity or a consortium of entities can potentially prevent an asset holder from transacting their cryptocurrency. This may be a simple denial-of-service (DOS) attack on the asset holder or on their ISP. Alternatively, it could be a more nefarious agreement among miners or block signers to not include the asset holder's transactions in blocks. This can be a very expensive problem to resolve, which means that the best solution is to make sure that no one knows who you are, and thus doesn't know who to censor.

Abstract Case Study: Extorting Funds. Frank is open about his bitcoin wealth and freely posts his contact info on bitcoin forums. He gets an email saying that his transactions will no longer be processed if he doesn't pay a consortium 1% of his bitcoin funds. Indeed, his transactions stop going through.

Historic Case Study: Blocking WikiLeaks. WikiLeaks was blockaded by several traditional financial institutions such as Mastercard, VISA, and PayPal in December 2010. Afterward, Satoshi Nakamoto is reputed to have asked WikiLeaks not to use bitcoins for donations, and some miners were reluctant to process WikiLeaks transactions. However, there wasn't sufficient consensus to extend the financial blockade to bitcoin. **News Story**[148], **Another New Story**[149].

---

[148]https://www.forbes.com/sites/jonmatonis/2012/08/20/wikileaks-bypasses-financial-blockade-with-bitcoin/#6a7803b47202
[149]https://www.coindesk.com/assange-bitcoin-wikileaks-helped-keep-alive/

Risks:

1. **Funds Denial.** Though the asset holder still has complete access to his key and thus exclusive access to his funds, he can't actually use them, so they might as well be lost (until something is done to clear up the censorship).

Process Solutions:

1. **Practice Anonymity.** Do not let people know you have bitcoins; ensure that you in no way ever link your key to your real persona.
2. **Practice Key Hygiene.** Follow the best practices of using different addresses for every transaction that you conduct. Each time you make a transaction with the same address, you are leaking information to your counterparty, which could be used to identify and either censor or correlate future transactions.
3. **Request Preferential Mining or Mine Your Own Blocks.** Gain control of some portion of the block creation infrastructure, most likely by purchasing enough mining power that you can occasionally generate a block. Of, more simply, pay a miner directly to mine your transaction.

Hot Wallet Solutions:

1. **Question Policies & Procedures.** Know the security policies and procedures of any company that you're working with; be sure that they have rigorous, well-documented security procedures that they follow religiously, and that they treat any variance from their procedure as a problem that must be investigated. Also, be sure that there are no negative policies that might affect your usage of its services.

See Related – Correlation.

Adversary: Correlation

Motivation. *"I want information. I watch cryptocurrency transactions with an eagle eye, ready to swoop in on any mistake. If you keep making the same payments or receiving the same payments or using the same addresses, I'll figure it out. I want to connect the dots to determine who is spending cryptocurrency for what, and I can figure that puzzle out if you give me enough pieces."*

Key Words: Active, Technological.

Cryptocurrency use is pseudo-anonymous and somewhat private. However, it's not totally so: it's possible to build up correlation. Through statistical analysis and through the discovery of accidental revelations, a third-party could tie together an asset holder's usage of various funds to paint a larger picture of their finances and contacts.

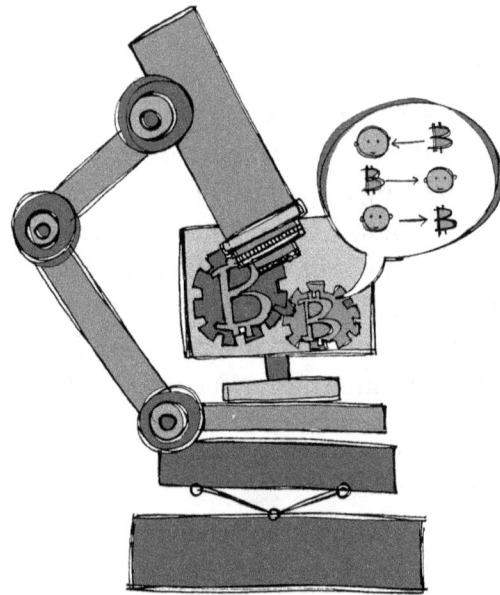

Abstract Case Study: Correlating over Coffee. Alice is sloppy with her bitcoins and tends to use one address for everything. She goes out to buy a coffee with bitcoins; while she sips away at the café, working at her laptop, the barista notes the huge number of bitcoins going into the address. She follows Alice home, planning larceny.

Abstract Case Study: Correlating Identities. Carol uses the same online identity on bitcointalk and on twitter. Eastern European hackers monitor twitter, see her talking about bitcoins, track that back to bitcointalk, and find wallet addresses mentioned there that reveal her bitcoin wealth. They then set their scripts lose, hoping to break into her computer and steal her keys.

Risks:

1. **Funds Revelation**. An asset holder's ownership of various funds can be revealed. This can make it possible to track what they spent funds on and who they're associated with. It also puts them in greater danger from any number of other adversaries.

2. **Cascade: Censorship**. If they know who you are, they can block you.

3. **Cascade: Coercion**. If they know who you are, they can threaten you.

4. **Cascade: Legal Forfeiture**. If they know who you are, you can become a target for a nation-state or for a civil action.

5. **Cascade: Loss of Fungibility**. If funds have been correlated, they may lose fungibility.

6. **Cascade: Sophisticated Theft**. If they know you you are, you can become a target for thieves.

Process Solutions:

1. **Practice Anonymity**. Do not let people know you have bitcoins; ensure that you in no way ever link your key to your real persona.

2. **Practice Anonymizing Your Funds**. Occasionally use methods like CoinJoin, SendShared, or Zerocoin to anonymize your transactions. On Blockstream's Liquid, always make use of Confidential Transactions.

3. **Practice Key Hygiene**. Follow the best practices of using different addresses for every transaction that you conduct. Each time you make a transaction with the same address, you are leaking information to your counterparty, which could be used to identify and either censor or correlate future transactions.

Adversary: Loss of Fungibility

Motivation. *"I want to figure out how your cryptocurrency has been used in the past. That way, I can decide whether to accept your funds based on their history. Maybe they were used for criminal activities or maybe they were stolen; I don't want to accept those tainted funds. Or maybe they were owned by someone I don't like, and I'm trying to punish people for transacting with them. Whatever the reason, it's vital that I be able to backtrack the history of your coins."*

Key Words: Active, Technological.

Fungibility presumes that all bitcoins (or other cryptocurrency units) are indistinguishable and interchangeable. This ensures that all currency has the same value: a bitcoin doesn't become more valuable because (for example) it was held by Satoshi or less valuable because (for example) it was used to pay for illegal activities. Unfortunately, the fungibility of Bitcoin is in danger because some exchanges and wallet services have begun using tracing services; worse, they have begun freezing accounts where they don't like their activities.

Abstract Case Study: Gambling with Funds. Dan stores his funds at an exchange. He uses some of them to try out a Bitcoin gambling site, and the next time he returns to the exchange he finds his account locked because he's violated a no-gambling policy that was created by the exchange to pacify the US Department of Justice.

Risks:

1. **Funds Denial**. The big problem with loss of fungibility is that the entire cryptocurrency ecosystem might become unwilling to accept a coin with a bad history.

2. **Key Loss**. More trivially, if you find your account locked by a particular exchange, you might lose access to keys generated by the exchange for a while.

Process Solutions:

1. **Practice Anonymizing Your Funds**. Occasionally use methods like CoinJoin, SendShared, or Zerocoin to anonymize your transactions. On Blockstream's Liquid, always make use of Confidential Transactions.

Hot Wallet Solutions:

1. **Create Cold Storage Procedure**. Adapt a **Cold Storage Procedure** that moves some or all of your funds off of your hot wallet. Only keep keys on an exchange or brokerage for the minimum amount of time required to make a transaction. *Dangers: Disaster, Casual Physical Theft.*

2. **Question Policies & Procedures**. Know the security policies and procedures of any company that you're working with; be sure that they have rigorous, well-documented security procedures that they follow religiously, and that they treat any variance from their procedure as a problem that must be investigated. Also, be sure that there are no negative policies that might affect your usage of its services.

Part Three: Fiduciary Duties

Early parts of this book focused on the simplest scenario: self-custody, where you're only holding your own digital assets. Many people will instead be holding assets in trust for other people, and this introduces a whole new level of fiduciary duty –Â one that is discussed in this last Part.

An overview of **Digital Custodianship Responsibilities** provides the barest summary of this complex area of law, acting as a starting place for anyone who needs to delve more into the topic of holding digital assets for other people.

The Frank Family Fund Example then offers an example of how the risk modeling methodology of this course can be to resolve vulnerabilities in a more complex custodian setup. Note that all of the topics discussed to date remain relevant: the same risk modeling system can be used, the same adversaries can be dangers, and the same cold storage scenario can be applied to assets that don't need to be in a hot wallet. The Frank Family Fund thus demonstrates how this course's material continues to be relevant to increasingly complex (and realistic) custodianship scenarios.

Chapter Four: Digital Custodianship Responsibilities

Caring for other peoples' assets

Version: 2018-09-21 1.0.0

Introduction to Fiduciary Responsibilities

Digital currency is a groundbreaking new asset class that allows for easier individual control and management of assets than previous classes. This has created a somewhat *laissez faire* attitude toward digital currency custodianship, even when it extends from personal ownership to custodianship of digital assets for family, friends, trusts, or customers. This is a grave mistake because digital custodianship requires the same high levels of faith, trust, and protection as any other asset that one might oversee and safeguard.

Generally, digital custodianship falls under **fiduciary law**. This is a lesser know type of law that rises to preeminence when one person (a fiduciary) holds some position of trust for another person (a client), particular when the fiduciary is holding money or property. In the case of cryptocurrency, a fiduciary holds digital assets for a client. Fiduciary law creates specific responsibilities that cannot be waived by *either party* even under a contract.

When a trustee holds a client's digital assets they must uphold a **fiduciary duty** in regard to those assets, acting in the *best interest* of the owner. The specifics of these duties vary from jurisdiction to jurisdiction, but it generally requires the "highest standard of care". Wikipedia offers a more extensive definition: *"When a fiduciary duty is imposed, equity requires a different, stricter ... standard of behavior than the comparable tortious duty of care at common law."*

These duties may include "duties of care", where the fiduciary is required to keep himself informed for the benefit of his client, and "duties of loyalty", where the fiduciary must put the interests of his client foremost and cannot act in his own self-interest. Duties of confidentiality, disclosure, good faith, and prudence may also be recognized. The *2003 SEC regulations*[150] are likely to apply most directly to the fiduciary duties of digital custodians.

Best Practices of Digital Custodianship

The wider financial industry has long practiced and defined the "different, stricter" requirements of fiduciary duty. One requirement regularly rises to the forefront and should also be considered a minimum level of care to support the fiduciary duty required by digital custodianship:

---

[150]https://www.sec.gov/rules/final/ia-2176.htm

Dual control requires that two people be present for certain sensitive financial operations. In the classic financial world, two employees might exercise dual control when transferring a cash drawer, while a banker and customer might exercise dual control to open a safety deposit box. In some cases, one of the controllers may need to be from outside the company, such as an auditor.

For digital custodianship, dual control can easily be represented with a multi-sig, which requires two or more people to sign off on cryptocurrency transactions. If a custodian is actively investing and transferring digital currencies, then a multi-sig could require the signatures of two people at the investment house, while if it's simply holding the cryptocurrency, it could require a signature of a custodian and their client.

A 2-of-2 multi-sig is the most obvious analogue to a physical dual-control scenario, but increasing the number of possible signers (without increasing the number of required signers) can reduce cryptocurrency's issues of key fragility. Generally, increasing the number of required signers will increase the security at the cost of fragility while increasing the the number of possible signers will decrease the fragility at the cost of security. A 2-of-3 multi-sig may be a good compromise, where any two people from a group of three can sign off on transactions. (Shamir secret sharing is another technical option for dual control, but is generally considered less secure due both to its single-point-of-failure when the key is reconstructed and to its apparent ease of implementation.)

Dual control in digital currency can also go beyond these simple technical means. It can (and should) be baked into other sensitive areas, such as the creation of scripts, which should be checked by at least two engineers as a general policy.

Dual control is built on the larger concept of *separation of duties*, which generally says that that different people should be involved in different parts of a transaction. This goes beyond simply protecting the most sensitive financial operations; it should be built into any digital custodianship as a best practice for all phases of operation.

Separation (or segregation) of duties can be best achieved by breaking down the lifespan of digital custodianship into its constituent parts. This includes phases like intake of fiat currency, intake of cryptocurrency, purchase of digital currency, sale of digital currency, transfer of digital currency, and transfer of fiat currency. Having different people responsible for some or all of these duties helps to ensure that neither fraud, incompetence, or accident is likely to impact digital currency custodianship.

Additional Requirements for High Value Accounts

Additional fiduciary requirements and responsibilities may apply when higher values of digital assets are held by a custodian. The SEC requires that the traditional Registered Investment Advisor (RIA) model use an external qualified custodian to hold amounts larger than $150 million. It remains unclear if these regulations apply to cryptocurrencies, as the SEC has said that Bitcoin and Ether are not securities.

However, digital custodians should carefully consider and reconsider their setup to see if a qualified custodian is suggested if they reach a $150 million plateau of value, which is very easy given the rapid upswings in cryptocurrency price that have occurred in the past. They should also keep abreast of local laws, state laws, or international laws that might regulate custodianship at certain high-value breakpoints.

References

"Breach of Fiduciary Duty Law and Legal Definition". USLegal.com. *https://definitions.uslegal.com/b/breach-of-fiduciary-duty*[151]

"Custody: Uncharted Waters for Digital Assets". FinOps Report. *https://finops.co/investors/custody-unchartered-waters-for-digital-assets/*[152]

"Custody of Funds or Securities of Clients by Investment Advisers". SEC. *https://www.sec.gov/rules/final/ia-2176.htm*[153]

"Dual Control". Money Services Business. *http://moneyservicesbusiness.com/risk-mgt/dual-control/*[154]

"Fiduciary". Wikipedia. *https://ipfs.io/ipfs/QmXoypizjW3WknFiJnKLwHCnL72vedxjQkDDP1mXWo6uco/wiki/Fiduciary_duty.html*[155]

"Fiduciary Duty". Cornell Law School: Legal information institute. *https://www.law.cornell.edu/wex/fiduciary_duty*[156]

"Separation of Duties". University of Washington. *https://finance.uw.edu/fr/internal-controls/separation-of-duties*[157]

"URGENT: Fragmented Backups Vulnerability". Bitcoin Armoy. *https://btcarmory.com/fragmented-backup-vuln/*[158]

---

[151] https://definitions.uslegal.com/b/breach-of-fiduciary-duty
[152] https://finops.co/investors/custody-unchartered-waters-for-digital-assets/
[153] https://www.sec.gov/rules/final/ia-2176.htm
[154] http://moneyservicesbusiness.com/risk-mgt/dual-control/
[155] https://ipfs.io/ipfs/QmXoypizjW3WknFiJnKLwHCnL72vedxjQkDDP1mXWo6uco/wiki/Fiduciary_duty.html
[156] https://www.law.cornell.edu/wex/fiduciary_duty
[157] https://finance.uw.edu/fr/internal-controls/separation-of-duties
[158] https://btcarmory.com/fragmented-backup-vuln/

Chapter Five: The Frank Family Fund Example

Using risk modeling for more complex custodianship

Version: 2019-01-16 1.0.0

Introduction to The Frank Family Fund

This example details how to use this course's risk modeling methodology for a more complex system of digital-asset custodianship: the Frank Family Fund. In this made-up example, Frank has created a Family Fund intended to benefit his children and grandchildren. In late 2016, his manager Faythe decided to make a purchase of bitcoins due to the doubling of its value over the previous year. She placed $6M of the Frank Family Fund's money into the cryptocurrency. Over the next two years, bitcoin value naturally increased in value by about 10x, and Faythe managed another 2x growth due to expert leverage and arbitrage. This portion of the Fund is now worth approximately $100M after various costs and fees.

Unfortunately, the infrastructure that Faythe has built up around the cryptocurrency holdings of the FFF is haphazard and (frankly) risky. Faythe manages it along with her CFO, Bob, and two interns, Chuck and Dan. Private keys are largely held by online exchanges, but those services are accessible through authenticated APIs on an Amazon Web Service (AWS) server, which the interns have used to automate the arbitrage of cryptocurrencies and the purchase and sale of options. Anyone in the office could probably do anything they wanted with the funds, and there's also considerable exposure at AWS and the other online services.

The FFF could easily lose everything, and so it's badly in need of some risk modeling.

Section I: Asset Characterization

Step 1: Identify Your Assets

Faythe's Story. The assets in the FFF are divided between three locations.

60% of the funds are stored at three different exchanges: Bitconnect, Bitfinex, and Binance. These exchanges were the foundation of the FFF's funds two years ago. As Faythe and her office gained experience with the money-making opportunities of cryptocurrency, they began using these exchanges for arbitrage: they purposefully maintain funds at different exchanges that support different pairings of cryptocurrencies, allowing for the quick purchase and sale of funds. Though the FFF occasionally dabbles in other cryptocurrencies in this way, it maintains most of its reserves in bitcoin or in Tether, with some Bitcoin Cash scattered across their accounts due to the fork. Authentication information for these accounts, which is used to automate arbitrage, exist on AWS.

20% of the funds are stored at Quedex, a bitcoin-settled options and futures market. This allows Faythe and her office to issue PUT calls for their bitcoin holdings as a hedge and also to further speculate on cryptocurrency futures using careful sets of PUT and CALL options. This has been a huge boon as bitcoin value has dropped in recent years. Again, these accounts are linked to the FFF's AWS server, to support automated creation and maintenance of options

20% of the funds are stored in cold storage. This is a haphazard collection of two Trezors, one Ledger, and a few dozen paper wallets that represent some early purchases and some attempts to move a percentage of funds to a less exposed medium.

Faythe initially writes down the crypto-assets in the FFF as follows:

1. Bitcoins in Exchanges
   a. Bitconnect
   b. Bitfinex
   c. Binance
2. Bitcoins, Options, and Futures at Quedex
3. Bitcoins in Cold Storage
   a. Keys in Hardware Wallets
   b. Keys in Paper Wallets

Faythe then realizes that she needs to write down one more asset: the AWS server that contains authentication for the exchanges and Qudex:

4. Authentication Info at AWS

Step 2: Value Your Assets

Faythe's Story. Faythe initially values Frank's assets based on the percentage of the FFF's value at each location, converting the percentagesages to a simpler number from 1 to 10:

1. Bitcoins in Exchanges [6]
    a. Bitconnect [2]
    b. Bitfinex [3]
    c. Binance [1]

Faythe notes that about 20% of the holdings are at Bitconnect, 30% at Bitfinex, and 10% at Binance.

2. Bitcoins, Options, and Futures at Quedex [2]
3. Bitcoins in Cold Storage [2]
    a. Keys in Hardware Wallets [. 5 = 1]
    b. Keys in Paper Wallets [1.5 = 2]

About three-quarters of the FFF's cold storage is old paper wallets, with the remaining minority being in high-tech hardware wallets. Though 1 + 2 don't add up to the overall 2, Faythe still feels that this is a good representation of the asset values.

4. Authentication Info at AWS [8]

Faythe had never realized how high the valuation was for that AWS account, but sure enough it gives comprehensive access to all of the exchanges and Quedex. Those represent 80% of the FFF's holdings, and they could all be lost if AWS was compromised, so she marks this as an 8.

Here are the final asset numbers for the FFF:

1. Bitcoins in Exchanges [6]
    a. Bitconnect [2]
    b. Bitfinex [3]
    c. Binance [1]
2. Bitcoins, Options, and Futures at Quedex [2]
3. Bitcoins in Cold Storage [2]
    a. Keys in Hardware Wallets [1]
    b. Keys in Paper Wallets [2]
4. Authentication Info at AWS [8]

Step 3: Diagram Your Process

Faythe's Story. Faythe decides to represent the FFF asset list as four nodes: the AWS cloud, the Bitcoin exchanges, the Quedex site, and the cold storage. Both the exchanges and the cold storage have subnodes, so she duly notes those too (though she expects to treat all of the exchanges as having the same vulnerabilities).

Because Faythe keeps careful records of everything, she didn't miss any physical nodes. She also decides not to include any alternate nodes at this point. At some time in the (hopefully) far future, Frank's funds will become available to his heirs, and some of them may want to cash out, but for now there are no fiat funds moving in and out of the system.

Faythe next draws out her interfaces. Most of them are just simple money exchanges, which run cash between cold storage, the Bitcoin exchanges, the Quedex site, and back. The FFF always uses the exchanges as the intermediary, because that's where the majority of the cash is. Faythe treats the interfaces leading into the exchanges ("fund exchanges") as all being the same, but recognizes that there might be unique vulnerabilities moving funds to cold storage and to Quedex.

The AWS cloud acts as the control for automated purchases and sales of both options and currencies, so there are interfaces from the cloud to both the exchanges and Quedex. Finally, there are internal interfaces for both the exchanges and Quedex that represent buying currencies (for arbitrage) and buying options. The options are mechanically simple, but the arbitrage is a complex system that involves simultaneously buying and selling currencies at two different exchanges, followed by a rebalancing of funds between the exchanges. Despite that complexity, Faythe decides to represent it as a simple "purchase currencies" interfaces, because that's the core action at each of the exchanges.

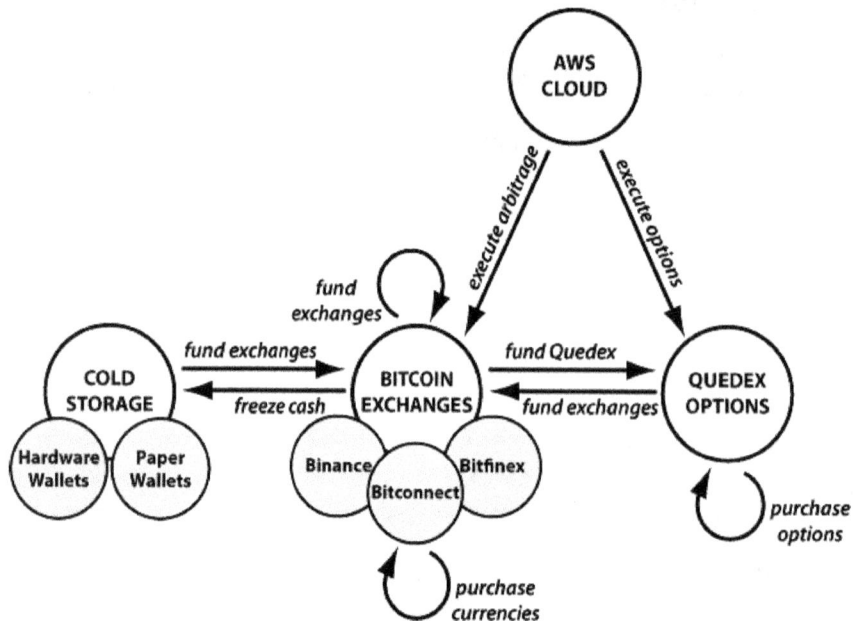

The end result reminds Faythe of the importance of both the AWS Cloud, which has considerable control over these cryptocurrency holdings, and the Bitcoin exchanges, which sit at the center of the diagram and connect to a half-dozen interfaces.

Section II: Risk Characterization

Step 4: Brainstorm Interface Vulnerabilities

Faythe's Story. Faythe numbers the interfaces and brainstorms vulnerabilities with Bob, Chuck, and Dan. Chuck seems disturbingly good at figuring out how things might break.

1. Freeze cash
    a. Paper wallet software did not generate a legitimate address
    b. I did not print paper wallet right
    c. I did not send to my paper or hardware wallet address
2. Fund Exchanges/Quedex
    a. I did not send to my exchange account
    b. Exchange did not record funds
3. Execute arbitrage
    a. I got bad data from exchange
    b. I sent command to wrong exchange
    c. My auth expired and I could not conduct arbitrage
4. Purchase currencies
    a. I purchased currencies too late
    b. I bought wrong currency
5. Execute options
    a. I got bad data from Quedex
    b. My auth expired and I could not purchase options
6. Purchase options
    a. I confused PUT and CALL options
    b. I choose incorrect expiry for options
    c. I choose incorrect strike price for options

As she writes her list, Faythe also notices that funding Quedex and the exchanges have the same vulnerabilities, so she collapses them into one interface.

Step 5: Brainstorm Custody Vulnerabilities

Faythe's Story. Faythe has a lot of different assets involved in the FFF cryptocurrency setup. She's the queasiest about the AWS node, because of its enormous control over her network, but she also realizes that those paper wallets are disasters waiting to happen.

7. Cold Storage: Paper Wallet
    a. Paper wallet is water damaged
    b. Paper wallet is burnt up in fire
    c. Paper wallet is thrown out as junk
    d. Paper wallet is stolen
8. Cold Storage: Hardware Wallet
    a. Hardware wallet stops working
    b. I forget Hardware wallet PIN
    c. Linked desktop software stops working
9. AWS
    a. My AWS node is targeted by hackers
    b. My AWS node is targeted by unethical employees
    c. My AWS node dies

Though the Quedex site and the Bitcoin exchanges will have different risk profiles due to their different asset exposures, they have largely the same potential problems, so Faythe lists them together:

10. Exchange (Bitconnect)
11. Exchange (Bitfinex)
12. Exchange (Binance)
    a. Company is targeted by hackers
    b. Bitcoins are stolen by employees
13. Quedex
    a. Company is targeted by hackers
    b. Bitcoins are stolen by employees
    c. Site problems prevent executing options in time

Step 6: Brainstorm Non-Physical Vulnerabilities

Faythe's Story. Faythe choose not to include any non-physical assets when she listed the FFF's assets in Step 2. There are certainly reputation concerns if she had a big loss of bitcoin. And, physical security is a general issue — but it goes far beyond her company's cryptocurrency holdings, so it's part of her larger risk model. She thus can skip over this step when specifically working through bitcoin risks.

Step 7: Assess Consequences & Likelihoods of Vulnerabilities

Faythe's Story. Faythe has a lot of vulnerabilities listed, 30 total, but she knows this is just the first step in winnowing everything down to the actual risks that she needs to really worry about. So, she writes down her total list of assets, interfaces, and related vulnerabilities and gets to work figuring out which ones are the most problematic.

She starts with the ***Consequences***. The assets (7-13) are easy, because they largely correlate with the values of the assets: in most cases, a vulnerability could result in the asset being entirely lost. There were just two exceptions, where vulnerabilities involve the automated software not making trades or purchases correctly (9c, 13c). That would certainly be bad for Faythe as a custodian and investor, but the actual loss of funds, even if this problem was ongoing for a long time, would be minimal when compared to the overall valuations.

The interfaces require Faythe to think more. When rebalancing funds, she never moves more than 10% of the fund's cash around at a time (1, 2), so again it would be very bad if that were lost, but it doesn't have the high consequence of some of the asset-related risks. Someday, if she were closing out cryptocurrency accounts, she might be moving more money and have to reassess this, but for the moment those interfaces get marked as low consequence. For the arbitrage and options (3, 4, 5, 6), Faythe sometimes quickly moves around up to 20% of the FFF's funds, so there are higher potential consequences there.

She then moves on to ***Likelihoods***. She opts to use the likelihood scale of: Very Unlikely (VU), Somewhat Unlikely (U), Possible (P), Somewhat Likely (SL), and Very Likely (VL). Obviously, this is a personal assessment, but by dividing things into these five categories, Faythe is able to meaningfully differentiate the vulnerabilities ... and if she's one category off, it's still meaningful. Though Faythe is a financial expert, she also has to assess the likelihood of whether her interns will make mistakes in their code or their understanding of the financial system.

When she's done, she has a chart of consequences and likelihoods for each asset and interface:

1. Freeze cash
   a. Paper wallet software did not generate a legitimate address [C: 1, L: VU]
   b. I did not print paper wallet right [C: 1, L: P]
   c. I did not send to my paper or hardware wallet address [C: 1, L: U]
2. Fund Exchanges/Quedex
   a. I did not send to my exchange account [C: 1, L: U]
   b. Exchange did not record funds [C: 1, L: VU]
3. Execute arbitrage
   a. I got bad data from exchange [C: 2, L: U]
   b. I sent command to wrong exchange [C: 2, L: U]
   c. My auth expired and I could not conduct arbitrage [C: 1, L: P]
4. Purchase currencies
   a. I purchased currencies too late [C: 2, L: P]

      b. I bought wrong currency [C: 2, L: U]

5. Execute options

      a. I got bad data from Quedex [C: 2, L: U]

      b. My auth expired and I could not purchase options [C: 1, L: P]

6. Purchase options

      a. I confused PUT and CALL options [C: 2, L: U]

      b. I choose incorrect expiry for options [C: 2, L: VU]

      c. I choose incorrect strike price for options [C: 2, L: VU]

7. Cold Storage: Paper Wallet

      a. Paper wallet is water damaged [C: 2, L: P]

      b. Paper wallet is burnt up in fire [C: 2, L: U]

      c. Paper wallet is thrown out as junk [C: 2, L: P]

      d. Paper wallet is stolen [C: 2, L: VU]

8. Cold Storage: Hardware Wallet

      a. Hardware wallet stops working [C: 1, L: U]

      b. I forget Hardware wallet PIN [C: 1, L: P]

      c. Linked desktop software stops working [C: 1, L: U]

9. AWS

      a. My AWS node is targeted by hackers [C: 8, L: SL]

      b. My AWS node is targeted by unethical employees [C: 8, L: U]

      c. My AWS node dies [C: 1, L: P]

10. Exchange (Bitconnect)

      a. Company is targeted by hackers [C: 2, L: VL]

      b. Bitcoins are stolen by employees [C: 2, L: U]

11. Exchange (Bitfinex)

      a. Company is targeted by hackers [C: 3, L: VL]

      b. Bitcoins are stolen by employees [C: 3, L: U]

12. Exchange (Binance)

      a. Company is targeted by hackers [C: 1, L: VL]

      b. Bitcoins are stolen by employees [C: 1, L: U]

13. Quedex

      a. Company is targeted by hackers [C: 2, L: SL]

      b. Bitcoins are stolen by employees [C: 2, L: U]

      c. Site problems prevent executing options in time [C: 1, L: P]

Step 8: Chart Consequences & Likelihoods to Reveal Risks

Faythe's Story. Faythe is now ready to chart out all the risks for the FFF.

As she does, she notices that her two axes aren't quite in alignment because her likelihoods are a 5-point scale and her consequences only went up to eight points, not the full ten. She could resolve this in two ways, either by just truncating the consequences, and having them run a little short, or by doing her best to make the five likelihood points and the eight consequence points take up the same amount of room; she does the latter. She plots in all her risks, then draws her risk-tolerance line at 70% (and an asymptotic curve at 20%).

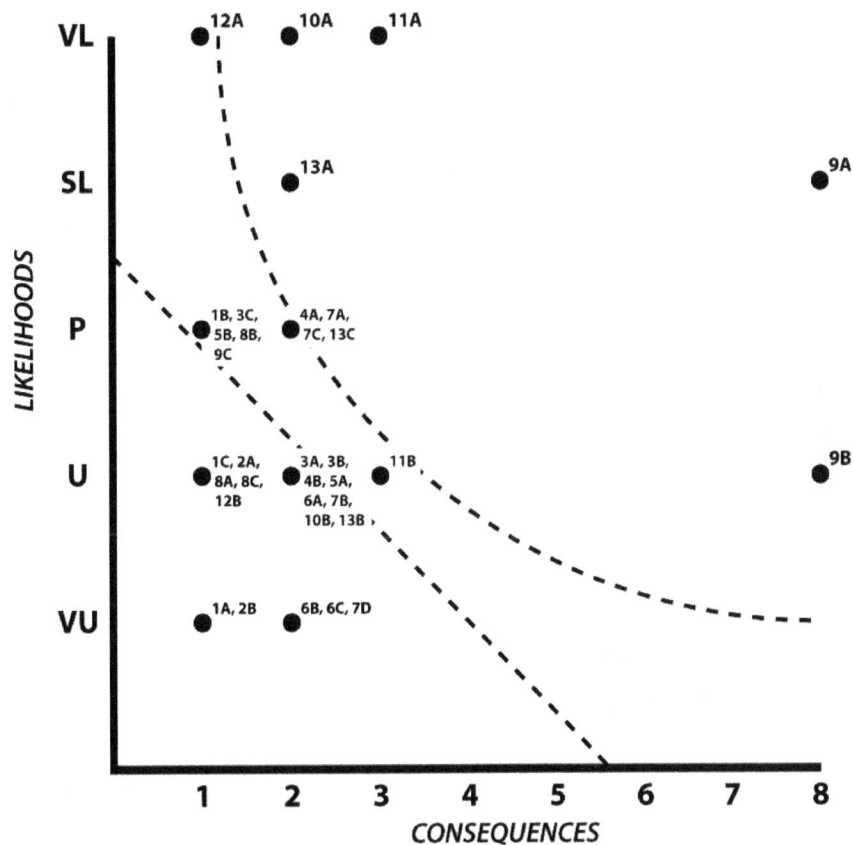

The overall chart looks pretty good. As Faythe suspected, the interfaces are the least of her problems. Safety for the FFF depends largely on her securing the places where assets are sitting.

Step 9: Consider Asset Valuation Changes

Faythe's Story. Before resolving risks, Faythe considers all of the FFF's assets in turn. She wants to know if they make sense, and if changing them could reduce risks.

First, up are the exchanges (10-12) and Quedex (13). Looking over the record of usage for the last year, she finds that the FFF usually uses all of the Quedex (13) and Binance (12) funds, but the Bitconnect (10) and Bitfinex (11) accounts are both overfunded: there are often bitcoins sitting there, not being used. So, she's going to reduce them by 10% each, with the excess going to cold storage.

This should put Bitconnect and Bitfinex closer to the risk-tolerance line and also drop the value of the AWS account (9).

This in turn raises the question of which cold storage to use, because it just creates more risk when Faythe must manage the potential issues of both hardware wallets (8) and paper wallets (7). Though Faythe rated the dangers of the two somewhat similarly, looking at all the options suggests that a hardware wallet is slightly better, so she consolidates on that. Doing so *will* raise some of the hardware wallet's dangers up to just over the risk-tolerance lines but it's a good tradeoff for the reductions in the danger of the online sites

1. Bitcoins in Exchanges [~~6~~ 4]
    a. Bitconnect [~~2~~ 1]
    b. Bitfinex [~~3~~ 2]
    c. Binance [1]
2. Bitcoins, Options, and Futures at Quedex [2]
3. Bitcoins in Cold Storage [~~2~~ 4]
    a. Keys in Hardware Wallets [~~1~~ 4]
    b. ~~Keys in Paper Wallets [2]~~
4. Authentication Info at AWS [~~8~~ 6]

Faythe also talks with Chuck and Dan about whether the functionality of the AWS node can be divided up, perhaps with arbitrage control and options control being operated by different servers. Dan starts working on it. When he's done, Faythe will be able to revise her risk structure again. For now, she charts out the updates the result from moving finances around:

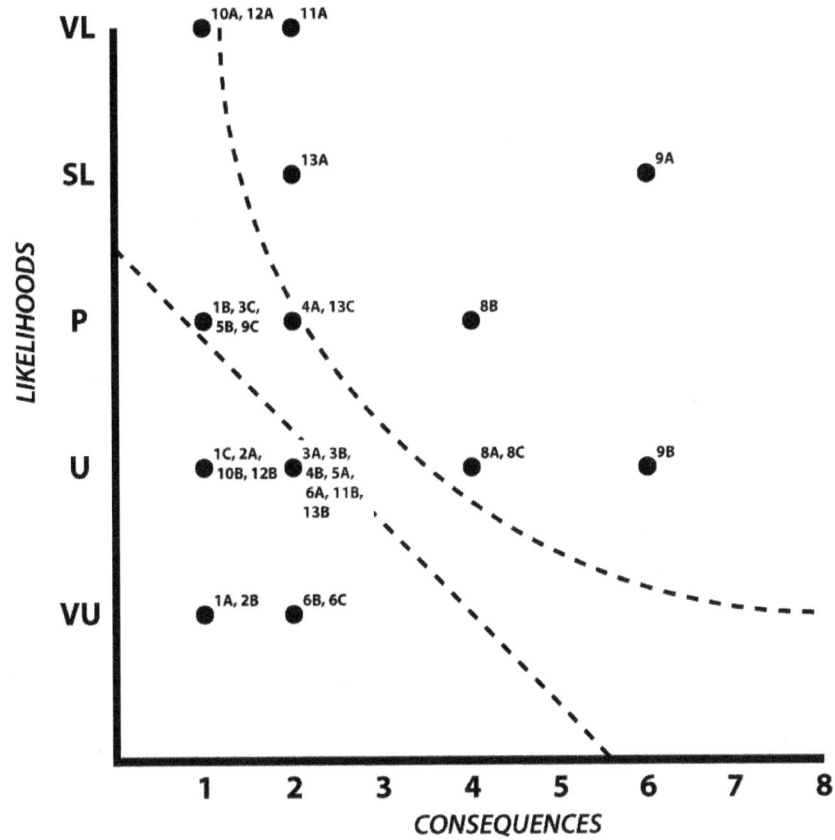

There are actually more risks above Faythe's risk-tolerance lines than there were *before* this step, but Faythe feels better with them as a whole, because everything is generally closer to the line.

Step 10: List Final Risks

Faythe's Story. Faythe now lists all the actual Risks revealed by her final chart. She explicitly includes the seven risks above both risk-tolerance lines and she explicitly excludes everything approximately even or both lines. That leaves her with ones in between the two lines. She decides the asset-related ones (10A, 12A) are very similar to other issues she'll be dealing with, and keeps them, but she doesn't worry about the procedure-related issues (4A, 13C).

1. 8A: Hardware wallet stops working
2. 8B: I forget Hardware wallet PIN
3. 8C: Linked desktop software stops working
4. 9A: My AWS node is targeted by hackers
5. 9B: My AWS node is targeted by unethical employees
6. 10A: Company is targeted by hackers
7. 11A: Company is targeted by hackers
8. 12A: Company is targeted by hackers
9. 13A: Company is targeted by hackers

Apparently, Faythe should be very worried about hackers, because the FFF has so much money in hot wallets and other online sites. That's reasonable.

Section III: Risk Resolution

Step 11: Correlate Final Risks to Digital Adversaries

Faythe's Story. Faythe now correlates her list to a set of standardized adversaries. In doing so, she realises that hackers can come in many forms.

1. 8A: Hardware wallet stops working — *Bitrot*
2. 8B: I forget Hardware wallet PIN — *Key Fragility*
3. 8C: Linked desktop software stops working — *Bitrot*
4. 9A: My AWS node is targeted by hackers — *Personal* or *Systemic Network Attack*
5. 9B: My AWS node is targeted by unethical employees — *Institutional Theft*
6. 10A: Company is targeted by hackers— *Personal* or *Systemic Network Attack*
7. 11A: Company is targeted by hackers — *Personal* or *Systemic Network Attack*
8. 12A: Company is targeted by hackers — *Personal* or *Systemic Network Attack*
9. 13A: Company is targeted by hackers — *Personal* or *Systemic Network Attack*

She then creates a prioritized list of adversaries to deal with:

1. Personal Network Attack [9A, 10A, 11A, 12A, 13A]
2. Systemic Network Attack [9A, 10A, 11A, 12A, 13A]
3. Bitrot [8A, 8C]
4. Institutional Theft [9B]
5. Key Fragility [8B]

This is a nice reduction from the 30 risks that Faythe initially laid out ... which is of course the point of the exercise.

Step 12: Take Steps to Foil Adversaries

Faythe's Story. Faythe now runs through all of the suggestions listed in her five adversaries, paying special attention to the Network Attacks, as the risk-analysis system listed them as her most important vulnerability. She ends up cutting out the "Institutional Theft" solutions entirely, because they're focused more on people stealing at her company than at the exchanges, and she doesn't consider that an issue based on her rigorous background checks.

Process Solutions:

1. **Maintain Emergency Procedure. (x2)**
2. **Monitor the Industry. (x2)**
3. **Monitor Your Funds. (x2)**
4. **Practice Anonymity.**
5. **Redundantly Relay Your Secrets.**
6. **Take the Time.**
7. **Verify Your Keys.**

For the process solutions, Faythe decides to concentrate on the first three, which showed up more than once. Emergency Procedures are exactly the sort of documented workflow that she wants to add to a process that grew up in an ad hoc manner. Meanwhile, regularly monitoring the industry and the FFF's funds should help to offset some of the implicit danger of having funds in hot wallets. She sets the interns on the latter: they'll spend some time watch Bitcoin news sources, and will also write some software to alert Faythe if funds suddenly change in an unexpected way.

Cold Storage Solutions:

1. **Backup Your OS File System.**
2. **Maintain Setup Information.**
3. **Physically Store Your Keys.**
4. **Redundantly Store Your Keys.**
5. **Rotate Your Key Storage.**
6. **Verify & Rotate your Backups.**
7. **Verify Your Key Storage.**
8. **Cold Storage Scenario and Optional Steps:**
    a. Use a (Second) USB Stick
    b. Use Bags (Tamper-Evident)
    c. Use Metal Enhancement (Redundant Metal Devices) **(x2)**
    d. Use a (USB) Laser Printer.

The cold storage solutions are an epiphany for Faythe. She'd previously thought of the paper wallets and Ledger as a fire-and-forget solution to store some bitcoins in a less exposed way, but now she realizes that they're full of dangers too.She sets the interns to adopting the entire cold storage procedure, with all the suggested optional steps. With Redundant Metal Tiles acting as a supplement to the Ledgers, Faythe no longer needs to worry about what would happen if she forgot the PIN, but simultaneously the PIN-locked Ledgers and the separated tiles provide excellent protection from any sort of casual theft.

Hot Wallet Solutions:

1. **Create Cold Storage Procedure. (x2)**
2. **Maintain Account Security. (x2)**
3. **Practice Session Security.**
4. **Question Policies & Procedures.**

Faythe knows that the hot wallets at the exchanges and Quedex represent the greatest vulnerabilities in the FFF's cryptocurrency scheme, but unlike many investors, she doesn't have the option to minimize that vulnerability, because she's an active trader in options and cryptocurrency alike.

Still, she can try to reduce the danger, and these solutions point the way. First, she tells the interns to regularly rotate the passwords and other authentication information. Second, she begins preparing questions for the exchanges to assess how they protect their bitcoins; if they won't answer or they give her answers that she doesn't like, then Faythe will consider other alternatives: there are a lot of exchanges out there, and at least she can choose the ones that are best secured.

Section IV: Process Repetition

Step 13: Repeat the Process

Faythe's Story. The biggest changes to come out of Faythe's risk-modeling work were procedural, informational, or related to the single node of cold storage. A few months later, Dan is also able to come up with a solution that allows splitting the AWS node without damaging the overall process that allows trading of both currencies and options.

Thus, Faythe's final diagram is a bit different from the original:

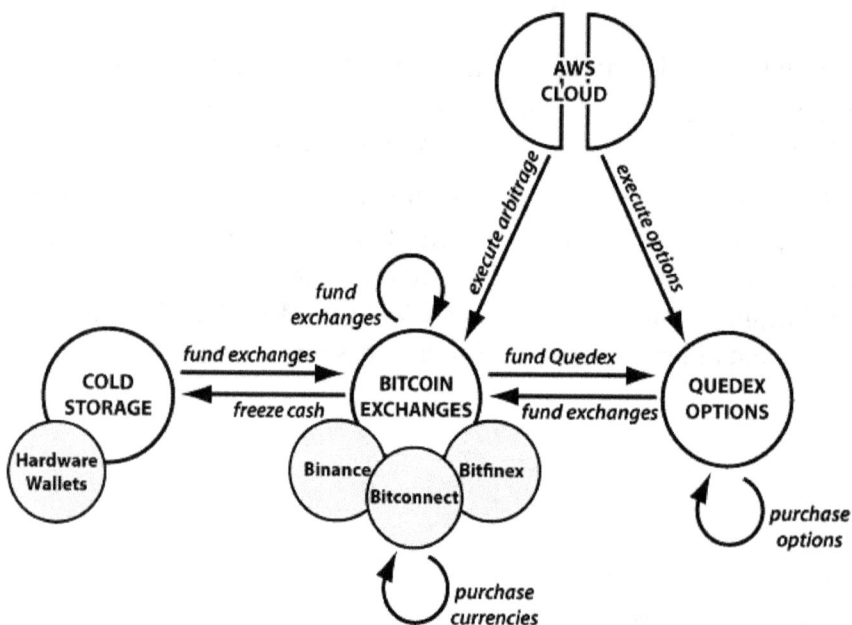

She'll use this new diagram as the foundation of a new risk-modeling exercise in 6-12 months time.

Appendices

References and resources

Version: 2019-06-27 Release 1.0.0

Appendix I: Sample Digital-Assets Letter

The following is a sample letter which could be used by a digital-asset holder to alert their heirs of the existence of the digital assets. For a more complete book on this topic, see Pamela Morgan's book Cryptoasset Inheritance Planning[159].

Dear [Heir],

Today's date is [Date]. This letter is intended to inform you that I own digital assets that are not held or controlled by third parties. I want to be sure that you can access them in case someday I can't. Do not access these digital assets unless I am dead or mentally incapacitated.

Please read through this letter completely before you take any action, and get the help of someone knowledgeable about digital assets such as [a trusted person or persons familiar with digital assets].

Remember, these assets aren't held by a bank and mistakes can't be fixed; the transfers must be done correctly or the funds could be lost forever. Closely watch everyone who helps and make sure you understand everything that is happening. Be extremely careful with PINs, passwords, and "wallet backups" because anyone who sees them can steal the digital assets.

To date I've used [digital-asset exchange brokerage] as my digital-asset-to-US-dollars exchange. This exchange account is connected to my [insert traditional bank name] [checking, savings, or brokerage] account ending in [last 4 digits of the account number]. My exchange account is registered with the account name [account name] and password is [reminder of a password that you previously shared with the Heir(s)]. As of the date of this letter, there are no funds in [brokerage]; I only move digital assets there for the briefest amount of time possible in order to exchange to/from US dollars. However, you may need to access [brokerage] just in case there are any funds there in-progress; to do so, you'll need access to my phone for 2FA (two-factor authentication) to move any funds away. The PIN on my phone is [PIN, or reminder of a PIN that you previously shared with the Heir(s)] and the app [app-name] will give you the code to authorize transactions with [brokerage]. If you

---

[159]https://t.co/hsLxiZdQya

need to sell digital assets to US dollars, I recommend you set up your own accounts rather than use my [exchange] account. In all cases, you should work with the companies by going through their processes to gain legal access to my account, as it may be illegal for you to use my account and password directly.

Most of my digital assets are held under my master secret, which is a computer-generated 24-word recovery phrase. These words are stored at [where they're stored, and an explanation of whether any additional work is required to decrypt them]. Be very careful with these 24 words as with them anyone can steal my digital assets. It is safer to use [a hardware device containing the private keys], which is located at [location]. [Include a photo of the device too.] It is secured by [PIN, or preferably, an clue of what the PIN is that the Heir will recognize]. Try using that first with anyone helping you move or exchange digital assets and leave the 24 words in the safety deposit box as a last resort.

As of today there are [number] kinds of digital assets stored under my master secret: [a list of what they are]. In the future there may be more or less. Using that master secret, the funds can be recovered from anywhere, but the easiest method is to use my [hardware device] and [software program], which is accessible through a USB stick stored with my other materials.

There may be some other 24-word keys or passwords at [storage location]. These may have smaller amounts of money for [other endeavors] or for lesser incidental use while I'm traveling.

[Discussion of non-digital assets or important accounts, such as brokerage and email accounts, may also be appropriate for such a letter.]

Signed, [Digital Asset Holder]

Author Bios

Christopher Allen is an entrepreneur and technologist who specializes in collaboration, security, and trust. He worked with Netscape to develop SSL and co-authored the IETF TLS internet draft that is now at the heart of secure commerce on the World Wide Web. More recently, he was Principal Architect at Blockstream, where he led blockchain standards efforts. Christopher is today co-chair of the W3C Credentials CG working on standards for decentralized identity and founder of Blockchain Commons. He also founded and facilitates the semi-annual Rebooting the Web of Trust design workshops, which have generated over 40 collaborative white papers about the next generation of internet privacy, security, and identity software.

Shannon Appelcline is a technical writer with expertise in blockchain, cryptocurrency, and digital identity who specializes in making technical concepts accessible. He has regularly written for Bitmark, Blockchain Commons, Blockstream, and Certicom, and his work has made the front page of Hackernoon. He is also the editor-in-chief for Rebooting the Web of Trust. In the non-technical sector, Shannon wrote a four-book history of the roleplaying field, *Designers & Dragons*, and recently co-authored *Meeples Together*, a study of cooperative game design, with Christopher.

Blockchain Commons Links

Blockchain Commons

https://www.blockchaincommons.com/[160]

The Blockchain Commons is dedicated to "Supporting Blockchain Infrastructure, Internet Security & Cryptographic Research". #SmartCustody is a Blockchain Commons project.

Blockcain Commons BTCPay

https://btcpay.blockchaincommons.com/[161]

To support the project, you can make one-time BTC contributions via our BTCPay server.

#SmartCustody

https://www.smartcustody.com/[162]

The #SmartCustody project is focused on "The use of advanced cryptographic tools to improve the care, maintenance, control, and protection of digital assets." Besides this book, #SmartCustody has also offered workshops.

The #SmartCustody Book

https://github.com/BlockchainCommons/SmartCustodyBook/tree/master/manuscript[163]

The entire #SmartCustody book is available in a Github repo. Feel free to make Pull Requests or post issues to help us keep improving it.

#SmartCustody BTCPay

https://btcpay.blockchaincommons.com/apps/r6JPAMd5pUed6x4iQChstkkUx3q/crowdfund[164]

To support keeping this book freely available to the public and to support continued updates as technology changesm you can make one-time BTC contributions via our BTCPay server.

---

[160]https://www.blockchaincommons.com/
[161]https://btcpay.blockchaincommons.com/
[162]https://www.smartcustody.com/
[163]https://github.com/BlockchainCommons/SmartCustodyBook/tree/master/manuscript
[164]https://btcpay.blockchaincommons.com/apps/r6JPAMd5pUed6x4iQChstkkUx3q/crowdfund

The #SmartCustody Email List

https://tinyletter.com/SmartCustody[165]

Sign up to receive occasional announcements about new and updated documents and #SmartCustody workshops and events.

---

[165]https://tinyletter.com/SmartCustody

www.ingramcontent.com/pod-product-compliance
Lightning Source LLC
Chambersburg PA
CBHW051214200326
41519CB00025B/7109